HOW TO BECOME A
HIGHLY INFLUENTIAL PERSONALITY

Disclaimer

This book is designed and written to provide knowledge, inspiration and motivation to the readers. The author has shared his own experiences as a word of wisdom. The tips and guidelines in this book are not intended as a substitute for counselling. The content of each chapter is the sole expression and opinion of the author. No warranties or guarantees are expressed. The reader must test every tip and guideline by themselves. The author suggests the readers to fine-tune the tips and suggestions based on their real-life experience, situation and requirements.

Please share your feedback on *satesshsingh@gmail.com*

Please do visit my website *www.satesshsingh.com*

Positively charged!

Satessh Singh
"How to become a Highly Influential Personality"

HOW TO BECOME A
HIGHLY INFLUENTIAL PERSONALITY

32 Tips to Change Your Life

Authored by

SATESSH SINGH

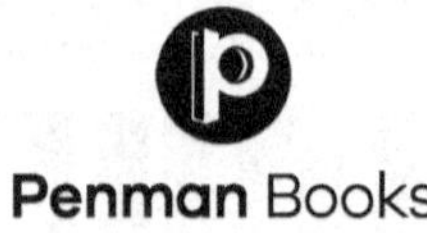

Penman Books

Office No. 303, Kumar House Building,
D Block, Central Market, Opp PVR Cinema,
Prashant Vihar, Delhi 110085, India
Website: www.penmanbooks.com
Email: publish@penmanbooks.com

First Published by Penman Books 2019
Copyright © Satessh Singh 2019
All Rights Reserved.

Title: How to Become a Highly Influential Personality
Price: ₹499 | $ 11.36
ISBN: 978-93-89024-31-9

Praise for the Author & Book

Amazingly crafted with very relevant and apt representations of new ways of looking into a polarised environment of work, life and managing oneself.

—**Rajib Das,** *Chief Marketing Officer, Sanzyme Ltd*

~~~

This book helps you to become a wise leader of your life journey.

—**Laura Dalla Valle,** *Senior Business Development Manager, Italy*

~~~

This book is about becoming a better person & is full of simple-to-understand, easy-to-implement tips. A breezy & easy read, a good addition to your collection.

—**Girish Mishra,** *Vice President, Zydus Healthcare Ltd*

~~~
~~~

"How to become a Highly Influential Personality" is a must-read. It's quick, its perfect and above all; its worth it and valuable.

—Anil Thomas,
Master NLP trainer n Gestalt Therapist

~~~

The beauty of this book is that it is the very simple-to-learn & understand. A person can follow the tips and guidelines to become his capable best and a highly influential personality.

—Nishith Shetty, *Director,*
Sharada International Hotels

~~~

The book has been written in Lucid manner and in the language a common person can grasp and adopt new qualities towards personality development.

—Dr. C V Achhra, *Former Principal &*
Director- CHM Campus

~~~

The author has given beautiful insight into the complex competencies with practical tools. It is a must-read for all entrepreneurs and professionals.

—Vijay Sonawane, *Career Coach*
~~~

Satessh has done a commendable job in simplifying into everyday language by using relevant examples. Many of the examples and their principles have direct applicability to today's business.

*—**Dr. Nitin Gore**, President Quality - Amoli Organics Limited*

~~~

"The ideas & tips in the book 'How to become a Highly Influential Personality' don't just make you effective but a much better person."

*—**Debashis Sarkar,** Founder & Managing Partner, Proliferator Advisory & Consulting*

~~~

The author Satessh Singh has cognitively simplified the process with positive tips.

*—**Leslie Rebelo,** Director- L. R. Associates Pvt Ltd*

~~~

One of the best books in the arena of self-development. The transformational chapters are short, effective and beautifully crafted keeping all the age groups in mind. If you are looking for a single self-help book that gives you loads of great ideas on how to improve all the areas of your life and achieve holistic success, this would be the one.

*—**Kuunal Kummar,** Actor/Screenwriter/Director*
~~~

The Most encouraging take-home message is to understand the Real meaning of VIP and CEO. For sure "A Must Read" to better understand the true aspect and meaning of "highly influential personality".

—***Aashish S Mangal,***
Founder- Pace Group of Companies LLC

~~~

The book beautifully explains the new meaning for the word CEO "Chief Encouraging Officer". This will help every CEO to be more creative like Satessh Singh.

—***Bharat Vishe,***
Managing Director- Vishe Education Pvt Ltd

~~~

The book promises an interesting journey dotted with real-life examples from the author's life and times.

—***Salil S. Kallianpur,*** *Founder & MD,*
ARKS Knowledge Consulting Pvt Ltd

The book 'How to Become a Highly Influential Personality' is one of the few books which can actually impart a lot of insights in a very short span of time in today's busy world.

—***Dr. Ashwini Kumar,***
CEO-CliniExperts Services Pvt Ltd

~~~
~~~

The book has many stories and incidents which will keep you glued to the book. Satessh is a maestro in storytelling. He makes the readers want to listen to him. This is a book worth its weight in gold.

—**Prof Vivek Hattangadi,** *Chief Mentor-The Enablers*

~~~

In his book "How to Become a Highly Influential Personality" Satessh Singh explains great ideas and teachings in simple, wise and practical ideas through thirty life-changing modules to achieve personal and professional greatness.

—**Upendra Singh,**
Senior Professional in Oil & Gas Industry

~~~

The book is filled with practical wisdom for people of all ages. The anecdotes and practical tips given are very powerful and enable the reader to enrich their professional and personal life. This book is a valuable addition to the literature of self-help in the present fast-paced life.

—**Colonel Vinay Gupta,**
Veteran- Indian Armed Forces

~~~
~~~

What a gripping, thought provoking and incredible book "How to become a Highly Influential Personality" written by Satessh Singh. This book will take you to a memorable journey of your life. You would be blown away with so easy to take actions. I would conclude with this to become influential personality do read this "MASTERPIECE".

—Parikshit Jobanputra,
Author, Motivational Speaker, Life Coach

~~~

After reading and applying the tips mentioned in the book, one can experience a transformed life.

—Nishit Lal, Author,
TEDx Speaker, Team Thought Bulb

~~~

One of the most striking features of the book is the uncompromising approach of its author. Everything becomes very clear and straight forward. "How to become a highly influential personality" depicts a huge energy charge.

—Hariram Krishnan,
Executive Coach & Mentor,
Former MD-Galderma India

Acknowledgements

I strongly believe that as an individual; we can't achieve something great in life without the inspiration, motivation, support, guidance and contribution of many like-minded people around us.

I admit to the importance and invaluable contribution of people who have inspired and motivated me to write "How to Become a Highly Influential Personality".

I am blessed to have received the best possible upbringing and values infused in me by my parents. My very special gratitude and thanks to my parents for always showering blessings upon me. I pray to God to gift me both of you as my parents in my next human birth too.

Every successful man has a great visible and invisible support from his wife. And I am not an exception! My wife Biindu pushed and pulled me to complete the book. My unlimited gratitude for her.

I am blessed to have two lovely and intelligent children. My daughter Ayushi and son Arryan, together they have contributed immensely as the best readers, critics, advisors and guiding forces in writing this book. Love you both.

I am also highly grateful to all my managers who taught, guided, sponsored and upgraded my knowledge and skills to achieve great success in my corporate life.

I am sure you would like the cover page of the book which is suggested by Ketan Khadse and finally designed by Neeraj Sharma and his team at Penman Books. Ketan, Neeraj and team- you all are awesome!

Though Nimesh Nayak was highly busy in his career but he contributed extraordinarily in crafting the manuscript.

It is said, "A great start is full done." God connected me timely with Tarun Singh and Neeraj Sharma my publishers who run Penman Books successfully. Tarun and Neeraj made my journey highly easy and smooth. God bless you both!

Parikshit Jobanputra, a renown life coach and India's No.1 Parenting Coach holds a very special place in my heart as he ignited me to write my first book. Thank you PJ!

I'm delighted to mention my gratitude to all the special personalities who read my book before publishing and shared their true and honest testimonials. These personalities are from different walks of life, like my college Principal, friends, well-wishers, corporate managers, entrepreneurs, business owners, academicians, actors-directors, trainers and coaches. I am genuinely grateful to

Nitin Datta and Arryan Siingh who have put in their best efforts to edit my book.

I dedicate all my work and glory to the Lord Ganesha.

My sincere gratitude to all who have helped me to write this book.

Foreword

"A much-needed and thought-provoking book indeed!

Being a part of academics now, especially in the area of making the Millennial's job worthy, this book "How to Become a Highly Influential Personality" is God sent!

Most professional courses impart knowledge, but its application is something that is missing in the syllabus.

Here comes the great utility of this book!

There are umpteen books that preach what is to be done, but miss out on the crucial 'How'!

Satessh, in simple steps and flow, using real-life incidents, captures the essence and, spells out what makes a person impactful & influencer!

Making the people feel important and heard intimately is what creates wonders in Relationships. Along with other critical traits, it brews in e.g. Punctuality, Active

Listening and Encouragement, which have been brought out beautifully in this book!

Happy reading to all.

My best wishes!

Sunil Chaturvedi
Director-Pharma Network
NMIMS University,Mumbai.

Dedication

This book is dedicated to the five most important people in my life for their never-ending love, support and encouragement in the realization of my goals and dreams.

My parents for being the most loving, caring and supporting parents any child could have asked for. My unlimited gratitude for everything you have done for me. I love you and miss you both.

Biindu, my loving and kind-hearted wife. You are my soul mate and best friend for the last 25 years. I feel blessed to have a life partner like you. My endless love and gratitude for being my soul partner. God bless us forever.

Ayushi, my daughter and Arryan, my son. I am a blessed and proud father to have both of you as my kids. You both make me complete, happy and a fulfilled father. You both keep me grounded as a human being. Love you both!

Introduction

I have invested 25 years in the Corporate world where I handled and orchestrated many departments like Sales, Marketing, Business HR, Supply chain, L&D.

However, when I came out of my college days, I had a tough start in the corporate career. I was unable to handle myself and the demand of the job. I used to struggle almost every day on account of managing relationships with my superiors, peers and juniors till I got promoted for the first time.

Soon, I realized the value and importance of an influencing personality and its outcome. Thereafter, I started acquiring knowledge and skills to become a charismatic personality.

I used to explore, experiment, design, implement, review and re-design my personality-influencing formulas. Steadily, I started enjoying the life of a highly influential personality. Due to my changed mindset, enhanced knowledge and sharpened skills about human psychology, my career took off like a rocket and I was rewarded with as many as fourteen promotions in just twenty years. I could realize that the biggest asset I had was human resource.

I started investing in my team and relationships. I started observing and re-aligning my response pattern. To my surprise, I started getting an amazing response. Gradually, I started experimenting, mentoring, sponsoring and elevating many young managers in all my corporate assignments.

I am pleased to mention that I had almost ninety percentage of internally promoted managers in all my projects. Today, all of them are highly successful, well-placed and happy in their life.

By now, many people started suggesting me to write a book based on an influential personality and share my gained knowledge with other people. I always dreamed of writing a book, so after a serious thought, I decided to write "How to become a Highly Influential Personality" which can help, guide and make youngsters a highly influential personality.

In this book, I have tried to share some of the real-life learnings and tips which are easy to apply, yet effective.

This book is not meant just to share information, instead, it is meant to transform. The book is written for young and aspiring generations who are either already successful or aspiring to become highly successful in their personal and professional life.

I have tried to quote in this book what has worked for me. I will refrain from making tall promises about the book. I want you to read and experience yourself. Only reading and experiencing is believing.

You may not agree with all of what I have shared in the book as many of the problems and their solutions may or may not be already be known to you. That is perfectly alright.

My suggestion to you is to focus on what is NEW and exciting for you. Choose and pick what works best for you and go ahead to apply and become a highly influential personality.

I have written this book straight from the heart. It would be worth if this book can add some value to your personality and finally in your life. I hope and pray that this book helps and inspires many youngsters to create an influential personality.

Since this is my first book, it is very close to my heart and hence I hope it finds a place in your heart too.

Wishing you a highly influential personality!

If you like any particular topic or idea or tips then please write to me your feedback on *satesshsingh@gmail.com*

I would love to listen from you.

Positively charged!

Satessh Singh
"How to become a Highly Influential Personality"

Contents

CHAPTER
One

Welcome to the World of
'Being Human'

I welcome each one of you to the new world of a Superhuman; the transformative world of ideal 'being human'.

Yes, you read that right! We are all evolved human beings but we need to ask a hard-hitting question to ourselves – are we an evolved Being Human? If the answer is NO then we must re-explore our behavior patterns and the way we deal with other human beings.

During our evolvement, we tend to ignore some of the key behavioral aspects in our day-to-day life.

So, let me welcome and congratulate you for joining this beautiful journey with me to your transform from human being to 'being human'.

However, before we embark on this life-changing voyage, let me answer a few questions for you.

Will this journey be an easy journey? Well, the answer is NO. Will this journey be an enjoyable one? The answer is BIG YES. Are we going to learn something new? The answer is NO. Are we going to explore something new? The answer is YES.

While being your pathfinder in this journey, I am committed to unfurl to you the exciting strength of a human being that we all have been gifted by the Almighty. However, many of us might have either forgotten or ignored the presence of this strength during our upbringing. I am going to peel off the human psyche layer by layer; like that of an onion.

There is a very distinct difference between Human Being and Being Human.

Human Being is a person who is distinguished from other animals or living species, whereas Being Human is simply understanding and respecting human values in other humans.

Being Human is an honest practice of humanity and kindness by respecting every human being's equal rights . Being Human is an art of treating people in a manner that boosts their Confidence, Self-esteem and Pride, the same way we expect others to treat us.

Being Human is giving space, respecting the privacy and allowing another person to put forward his/her point of view without creating any conflict or heartburn.

Being Human is extending core human values to the other person. For this, we need to put ourselves in the other person's shoess to know and understand his/her point of view.

> *Being Human is a great way to*
> *deal with Human Beings*

💡 GOLDEN NUGGETS ──────────────────

- *There is a very distinct difference between a Human Being and Being Human*

- *Human Being is a person who is distinguished from other animals or living species*

- *Being Human is an honest practice of humanity and kindness by respecting every human being's identity*

- *Being Human is giving space, respecting privacy and allowing another person to put forward his/her point of view without creating any conflict or heart burn*

CHAPTER
Two

Treat People like a VIP

You would agree that we like to be treated like a VIP – a Very Important Person, so do the others. Therefore, the first thing we must give utmost importance to is the other person. We must make them feel like a VIP.

The moment the other person feels like a VIP, he is open to connect with us.

Majority of the time, people shut their minds if they don't get importance and comfort in dealing with us. They expect us to treat them like a VIP. The moment we treat them like a VIP, half of our job is done.

So, how do we treat another person like a VIP? Simple. Greet them with a smile! Show warmth! Be original! Be genuine! Exhibit transparency! Be patient! Listen to them attentively! Lean towards them while interacting! Be empathetic! Never confront! Never criticize!

Hotel Sayaji is a very good value-for–money. This hotel is located in Indore-India. They have a very special as well as a unique way of treating their guests. The moment you get down at the Indore airport, they pick you up on a shared basis (if you have booked the complimentary pickup and drop service). They escort you to the pickup car and offer you a bottle of water and some tissue.

Also, they hand over the keys of your hotel room in the car itself. The moment you check–in, you will find your room doors open to welcome you in. Their staff doesn't accept any kind of tips as they proudly wear a badge that reads, "Please don't tip us, we will apply you service charges." What a way to treat the guest! I found ultimate 'customer delight' and again a smooth check-out and drop service to the airport.

Similar was my experience in Hotel Del' Annapurna at Darbar Marg in Kathmandu-Nepal, where I have been a regular guest for the past one decade. I haven't changed this hotel for the last ten years. The reason being; I have always been treated like a VIP in this hotel.

I am sure you also must have felt delighted as and when someone treats you like a VIP!

These kinds of treatments will always give you a VIP feeling.

Remember, when we treat other people like a VIP, they treat us the same way. It's the Law of Nature; *the input determines the output. What we give to Nature comes back to us in abundance.*

When you treat someone like a VIP, he/she carries positive and unforgettable memories about you. You become a permanent resident inside their heart.

What goes into Nature comes back to us. If we transmit negativity then we get negativity but if we send out positivity then we get back positivity.

However, to put forward our complete message, the communication has to be two ways. For dialogue to take place, one has to be open to listening to us and for that first, we must listen to the other person carefully and actively.

Most people like to be treated as a first-class category. Nobody likes to be treated like a second-class citizen. But when there is a wide gap between the expectations and delivery then we feel unhappy, frustrated, irritated, ignored and less important.

When we treat people well; they feel uplifted, they feel motivated, they feel excited, and they are recharged because they haven't received similar service from others.

Eventually, they carry a sweet memory about us. We create a very positive image in their mind. Therefore, to leave a lasting impression, it is significant that to create a very strong reputation in the mind of others.

> *"Experience leads to a belief; a negative experience triggers negative belief and a positive experience hatches positive belief."*
>
> **—Satessh Singh**

When we treat others like a VIP (Very Important Person), we feel like a VIP (Very Inspired Person)

💡 GOLDEN NUGGETS ──────────────

- *The moment the other person feels like a VIP, he is open to connect with us*

- *The input determines the output. What we give to the Nature comes back to us in abundance*

- *When you treat someone like a VIP, he/she carries positive and unforgettable memories about you. You become a permanent resident inside their heart*

- *What goes into Nature comes back to us. If we send negativity then we get negativity but if we send positivity then we get back positivity*

- *Everybody wants to be a first-class citizen but when there is a wide gap between expectations and delivery then we feel unhappy, frustrated, irritated, ignored and less important*

- *When we treat people well they are uplifted, they are motivated, they are excited, and they are recharged because they haven't received similar service*

- *Treating others like a VIP (Very Important Person) makes us also a VIP (Very Inspired Person)*

CHAPTER
Three

Be a CLO -
Chief Listening Officer

Agree not to disagree.

Yes friends, you read it right. If you wish to become a Highly Influential Personality then you should meet and greet people with an open heart and an empty mind (not a blank mind).

Never develop any assumption or presumption about people whom we meet. We have been conditioned since childhood to read a person as per our convenience, but when we read a person knowingly or unknowingly, we develop a fixed mindset about that person. We are biased towards that person. We are not open-minded. We are not open-hearted.

We love to hear what we expect to hear. However, this could be a big hurdle in attracting a person. The golden rule is, carry an open heart and an empty mind. Let's not become pre-conditioned. Try to have a heart-to-heart conversation and not a mind-to–mind one. The mind always tries to read and judge. The mind plays a game of intellectual.

Listen actively, get involved, get engaged, be curious, be intuitive and allow other people to speak, speak and speak. That is why God has gifted us a set of ear so that we can listen more and more.

Remember, you are not playing the fastest finger first, so no need to press the button without listening to the other person completely. Listen till the other person continues speaking. Don't interrupt him. Let him complete.

Once I joined a very famous company as their Business Head. Immediately after joining, the first briefing I got from my HR Head and my direct reportee about the sales team was "All the sales team are highly unionized and they don't work." This was a very scary feedback for me on my first day.

What I did was, first I started travelling and meeting all the senior people who were in the organization for more than 10 years. I was eager to meet them and know them personally and so were they. I remember distinctly when I met a few of them and allowed them to speak, they were hyper in the first few hours or so and after that, they were open to listen and follow what I suggested them. The important message here is "I listened to them carefully. I agreed to their points which were valid and genuine and beneficial to the organization too. After that, I also expressed the organizational expectations which they not only agreed to but also implemented those. That turned around the company's performance over a period of next six years till I was heading the business.

The feedback which I received was completely different and positive as compared to what I had received initially. What had changed? Nothing. All I did was listened to them, agreed and accepted some of their valid and genuine concerns. I made them agree to our genuine concerns. Thereafter, there was zero union issue in that organization till I served them.

Hence, we must agree not to disagree.

As a human being, for the majority of time, we hear and we don't listen. What is the difference between hearing and listening? While hearing, we don't absorb information, we don't connect with people and the topic. But when we listen; we process, we absorb and store the information which enables us to connect with people and the topic.

So, the best option is to listen actively and attentively. Be curious and intuitive while listening. We must listen to people to respond and not react. Allow people to open up and share their pain points.

"Hearing is temporary but listening is permanent."

—Satessh Singh

Remember, in communication what we absorb is more important and critical than what we talk.

We prefer not to agree and not to accept but we must learn and practice to agree and accept the other person's viewpoint without doubting them. This will help us in connecting with the other person.

Be an explorer. Be a digger. Be a surfer. Be a searcher. Be an inquisitive person. Be a curious man.

The moment we start listening to other people, they start connecting with us. It's magical! Try it. It works!

Remember, today we are living in an era of connectivity and networking. Hence, we must remain connected. People who are networking are ahead in their life.

Accept people as they are. Never try to change them. That is not your job. Instead, try to influence them. You are not a social reformer. Let them be happy in their own world. You must focus on becoming the most influential man. Extract the best from them and give the best to them. Be fair in your deal. Run an exchange offer which is win-win for both the parties.

Does it mean you need to sacrifice your own value system? The answer is NO. In creating a healthy chemistry, you do not have to tolerate nonsense. You need not have to deprive yourself of the deserving benefits.

Hence, you ought to be FIRM but be POLITE.

Politeness doesn't mean you can't protect yourself. Politeness means you are decent with a logic. Firmness means you are protecting yourself with a rationale. We need to be firm at our end without affecting our ethical core values. Never ever get influenced by a negative influencer. Protect yourself.

"Become a CLO – Chief Listening Officer."

—Satessh Singh

💡 GOLDEN NUGGETS

- *Agree not to disagree*

- *Try to have a heart-to-heart conversation and not a mind-to-mind one. Mind always tries to read and judge*

- *Listen actively, get involved, get engaged, be curious, be intuitive and allow other people to speak, speak and speak*

- *As a human being, for majority of time we hear and we don't listen*

- *While hearing; we don't absorb information, we don't connect with the people and the topic but when we listen; we process, we absorb and store the information which enables us to connect with people and situation*

- *Be an explorer. Be a digger. Be a surfer. Be a searcher. Be an inquisitive person*

- *The moment we start listening to other people, they start connecting with us. It's magical*

- *Extract the best from them and give the best to them. Be fair in your deal*

- *Politeness means you are decent with a logic*

CHAPTER
Four

Be Punctual

Being punctual is the mantra to a successful life.

Punctuality is a sign of professionalism. It helps you stand out as the most reliable and trustworthy person. Punctuality means always being on time for others.

Punctuality gives confidence to other people that you respect their time. It is based on two important factors. The first is respect for time and the second is respect for another person. Punctuality indicates seriousness, preparedness, alertness and value for the other person's time.

Punctuality is an attitude which demands will power and determination.

Punctuality shows you are genuinely interested. It is not only about being on time but it is basically about respecting your own commitments.

Whenever you are planning to meet somebody, always keep a buffer time to reach the location. You can't reproduce or recycle the lost time.

Habitual lateness symbolizes "My time is more valuable than yours" but habitual 'on promptness' evinces "Your time is more valuable hence I respect being on time."

I remember one of the episodes of my life when I missed my daughter's Graduation ceremony. It was 2nd August 2019, a Friday in Mumbai. It was the day when my daughter Ayyuushi was destined to receive her graduation degree on her Annual Convocation Day after investing her 5 years of hard work and dedication. I was excited and was waiting for this big day. I was yearning to attend the ceremony along with my wife and younger son. It was raining heavily in Mumbai since morning, so to avoid the traffic and parking hassles, we decided to travel by a radio cab. Unfortunately, it was pouring cats and dogs. The traffic was getting crazy. The car was hardly moving ahead. We were getting inquiry calls from our daughter again and again as she was anxious about her turn and doubted whether we would reach on time or not. She was getting panicky and so were we. Traffic was not at all easing out. We were hopeless. The heavy rain was continuously on and on and the traffic surrounding us stood still.

Our daughter informed us that the convocation program had started. We felt helpless and frustrated as we all waited for 23 years to witness this great day of our daughter's great achievement. Suddenly, we got a call from our daughter and she told us that she was going to share a link where we could see the live broadcasting of the convocation ceremony. We were a little relieved and at peace though witnessing the event in reality would have been a great experience to cherish throughout our life.

The learning I got from the entire episode was worth a million dollars. If the event was so important for us we could have reached the venue well in advance by keeping a buffer time which not only would have prevented us from unnecessary stress, anxiety and guilt but also would have given great happiness to our daughter and the entire family. Our daughter would have felt very special that day knowing how much we love and care about her.

This was the lost opportunity for me to say "We love you" "We care for you" "We are always there for you". Can I compensate this opportunity to express our love and affection to her? The answer is no. Many a time, we miss this kind of opportunity to express our love and care for the other person if we are not responding on time, if we are not punctual and if we delay.

I am sure you must have experienced a great degree of happiness and comfort whenever you were on time compared to whenever you were delayed. The delay would have wormed anxiety, lack of confidence, uneasiness, poor memory and poor thought connections.

The best suggestion here would be to always report fifteen minutes before the scheduled time. Keep some buffer time so that you reach before the other person does. Always refer to the traffic trends of the city or town.

You need to become a 'Time Thief' in order to organize your thoughts and align your agendas so that you connect all your dots in a much stipulated time.

When you reach the meeting point on or before time, you have already won the heart of the other person.

In fact, if the other person is delayed by a few minutes then he would surrender himself to you. In such case don't be reactive but try to understand the genuine reason behind the delay.

Give benefit of the doubt to the other person.

William Shakespeare beautifully wrote, "Better three hours too soon than a minute too late."

It is difficult to prove yourself reliable when people are forced to wait for you. Waiting for somebody is a crime. It is irritating and many times frustrating too.

It is said that the habitually punctual people make all their mistakes right on time.

"Punctuality should be way of life."

—Satessh Singh

GOLDEN NUGGETS

- *Punctuality is a sign of professionalism. It helps you stand out as the most reliable and trustworthy person. Punctuality means always being on time for others*

- *Punctuality is an attitude which demands will power and determination*

- *Punctuality shows you are interested*

- *You need to become a 'Time Thief' in order to organize your thoughts and align your agendas so that you connect all your dots in a much stipulated time*

- *Give benefit of the doubt to the other person*

- *Waiting for somebody is a crime. It is irritating and sometimes frustrating too*

- *Punctuality should be way of life*

CHAPTER
Five

Be a CEO -
Chief Encouraging Officer

Yes, you ought to become a CEO – Chief Encouraging Officer in your personal and professional life.

Everybody loves to be encouraged and appreciated. Allow the other person to empty his/her heart and mind. Don't interrupt him/her.

Keep asking questions while interacting. Allow the other person to talk and share. You just keep listening, encouraging and encouraging.

Nod your head positively when you find something interesting and exciting. Lean towards the other person. Show genuine interest. Show that you are excited to listen to their story.

Remember, everybody likes to be a speaker and share the story. Here, the speaker is the other person. So encourage them to empty out their heart to the fullest. Appreciate every good thing shared by the other person. Keep encouraging them genuinely.

Keep encouraging other people because your words may be the only tonic they must be looking forward to bounce back. Encouraging is another form of helping someone. The other person might find your encouragement as life-saver and morale booster.

I wish to reproduce an interview of an Indian legendary actor, producer, comedian and director Mehmood. In one of his interviews in Shekhar Suman's chat show Movers & Shakers, Mehmood shared with the audience how the current Bollywood icon Amitabh Bachchan struggled to dance in a song and gave up in the movie called Bombay to Goa. Later Mehmood asked his crew members, dance director and other co-actors to appreciate and encourage Amitabh Bachchan to extract the best from him. Mehmood shared that Amitabh Bachchan was highly nervous to do that dance sequence but due to tremendous encouragement and motivation infused by Mehmood and his other team members, he could give the best shot and the song is still an all-time superhit. It is still played in every dance party where people imitate Amitabh Bachchan's signature dance steps.

What a great thinking by Mehmood at that time! What a way to encourage and motivate Amitabh Bachchan.

In true sense, Mehmood played the role of a CEO – Chief Encouragement Officer. He simply extracted the best out of Amitabh Bachchan.

When you cheer somebody up, people feel encouraged. They feel you care about them. Inspired people always give their best. They outperform.

When you meet someone, appreciate their dressing sense, their smile, their overall appearance, their appointment, promptness and finally appreciate their efforts to meet you.

Be empathetic towards other people. Show your gratitude. Compliment them. Accept them as they are.

Use these sentences more often: "I really appreciate it" "That's very kind of you" "You are the best". These are powerful energy boosters that will infuse unlimited encouragement in the other person. Be a Chief Encouraging Officer.

When you encourage somebody they feel more relaxed, comfortable and inspired, thereby they open up naturally and easily. When a person opens up then he/she speaks more clearly and transparently. Connectivity and networking become stronger and more natural.

You will agree that encouragement is the key to any relationship. When you appreciate somebody, they feel good about what they do and they attempt to give their best. It adds new vim and vigor to strengthen the relationship further. Encouragement of any kind inspires people to outperform and bind strongly.

When you encourage people, they try to give their best in the shortest time so it's a jackpot for you also.

When you appreciate someone, it shows you are happy and delighted which in turn makes the other person happy, delighted and motivated.

> *"Be a CEO – Chief Encouraging Officer."*
>
> **—Satessh Singh**

GOLDEN NUGGETS

- *Everybody loves to be encouraged and appreciated*
- *Encouraging is another form of helping someone who finds it as life-saving and a morale booster*

- *When you cheer somebody, they feel encouraged. They feel you care for them*

- *Encouraged people always give their best. They outperform*

- *When you meet someone, appreciate their dressing sense, their smile, their overall appearance, their discipline and energy*

- *Be empathetic towards other people. Show your gratitude. Compliment them. Accept them as they are*

- *When you appreciate somebody, they feel good about what they do and they attempt to give their best*

- *Any kind of encouragement can prove to be a tonic to inspire people to achieve more*

- *When you appreciate someone, it shows you are happy and delighted which in turn makes the other person happy, delighted and motivated*

CHAPTER
Six

Have an Attitude of Gratitude

The attitude of gratitude has countless benefits.

*"Gratitude is a powerful process for shifting your
energy and bringing more or what you want in your life.
Be grateful for what you already have and
you will attract more good things."*

—Rhonda Byrne,
Author of the bestselling book "The Sectret"

It is human nature to like and respond to people who appreciate us and show us their gratitude.

Be grateful to people, expess your gratitude through a few kind words or some kind of gestures and you can be rest assured that it will come back to you in many folds.

Always be grounded and humble. Use more of 'please' and 'thank you' and other appreciative words that everybody likes and appreciates. Be thankful to the Almighty. Be grateful to your parents. Show your gratitude towards your family, friends, relatives, teachers, peers, seniors, customers, Nature and the entire Universe.

Sunil Gupta is the owner of a chain of hotels and resorts in Lonavala - a hill station near Mumbai city. Once he shared that 14 years ago he had a tough time to fulfill his family's basic day-to-day needs. He worked in some showroom in Pune before shifting to Lonavala to take up a job in a residential hotel. He is a great example of hard work. He has a magnificent business acumen, magnetic team retention ability, outstanding hospitality and a person with great value for gratitude. Sunil has developed a great attitude of gratitude. He always wears a smile on his face and greets everyone with folded hands. Irrespective of the stature of the other person, he treats everybody like a VIP. He is a true practitioner of "**atithi devo bhavah**" (In India we treat Guest like God). In the last 5 years, I have never seen him losing his contagious smile. I have never seen him losing his temperament. Today, he is the owner of more than a dozen hotels. Fifteen hotels in just fifteen years. Amazing growth!

Once I asked him "How do you manage such an attitude of gratitude?" He replied " Gratitude is the essence of my life. Today, whatever I have achieve is all because of my team and customers." How sweet of him! What a humble way of dealing with internal and external customers. Many of his current team members are from his first project. Nobody leaves him.

He always exhibits a great degree of gratitude towards his employees, customers and vendors.

The take-home learning for me was- always be humble, grounded and show gratitude; not attitude. Gratitude makes you a genius.

Aditya was my Head Sales HR. He was a great Business HR Manager. Once when I was shifting my family from another city to Mumbai for my new assignment. I was searching a good house in a good location which has all facilities like school, college, market and shopping malls. It was our financial year-end in February and March. Therefore, I was travelling extensively to close the financial year on a high performing note. He was playing the role of my real estate consultant at that point in time. I used to conduct my official tour and he used to search, shortlist and show me those options on weekends. He might have shown me more than a dozen options before I could finalise and lock a great brand new property in the most deserving residential complex of the area. Was he paid to do this job? Of course not. Was he compelled to do that? No. It was his kindness to help, support and make me absolutely comfortable so that I could focus on my business. I used to call him a business HR partner. He was a great practitioner of the human relations manager. He arranged my family's stay in a company guest house where my family stayed for almost three weeks before we shifted to our rented house. By that time, our new financial year had started and I was again travelling extensively. It was such a great experience for me and my family which we still cherish.

We are really grateful and thankful to him from the core of our heart.

Aditya, God bless you for your great care. Please accept my gratitude.

From the above real-life example, I learnt how to give importance and happiness to people when nobody is noticing or caring about them. Be selfless and enjoy the joy of giving.

 ## GOLDEN NUGGETS

- *The attitude of gratitude has countless benefits*
- *Always be humble, grounded and show gratitude; not attitude*
- *Give importance and happiness to people when nobody is noticing or caring about them*
- *Be selfless and enjoy the joy of giving*

CHAPTER
Seven

Respect People and their Sentiments

Dale Carnegie beautifully mentioned in his book that the sweetest thing to any human being is their name. When you meet someone for the second time and if you pronounce their name, they feel happy and delighted.

When you take some one's name, they feel that they are respected. They are loved. They are remembered. You care for them. Amazing feeling. Try yourself. It has a magical effect.

For my corporate stint, I travel more than 250 days in a year. I make it a point to call every person by their name. People feel very happy and delighted when I call them by their name. Similarly the cab driver, CISF Officers at Airport or Check-in staff of airlines; the moment I approach them, I read their names from their badge displayed on the left side of the chest (common sense). Every time I wish them, I could see a smile and spring of happiness on their faces.

The great Indian Space Scientist and ex-President Dr. APJ Abdul Kalam once said in his interview "Whenever I give any kind of happiness to anybody I feel happy and satisfied." What a noble thought! I fully agree as I have experienced the joy of giving myself.

Happiness is happiness. There is no measuring unit for happiness. No less or more or small or big happiness. Happiness is happiness.

Once, while entering the airport, I took a CISF Security officer's name at the entrance of the airport and to my surprise, I found he was highly delighted and touched by my behavior. Immediately, he looked at me, smiled and reciprocated to my wishes with full energy. He continued expressing his gratitude untill I entered the airport. That was an eye-opener for me and I decided to use the same formula to wish each and every staff who were doing the luggage screening and check-in. I was amused to see that, I made many people happy and made them feel like a VIP on that day. In return, they expressed gratitude to me.

Remember, the sweetest thing for any human being is their name. Therefore, calling them by their name with respect will boost up their dignity. Always call people by their first name. A human being loves their own name the best. We love to be called by our names.

Be humble and be down to earth which will take you to the greater heights.

When you are thanking people, please be genuine because people can make out whether you are genuine or a fake.

Similarly, when you are apologetic, be honest and sincere in your expression so that other people get tremendous psychological pressure to acknowledge your apology.

The heaviest thing to hold is a grudge. Hence, never ever keep a grudge against anybody. Forgive and forget.

A man grows in their stature when they offer an apology.

Feel empathy towards others. Empathy means caring and sharing.

When you pardon people, you win their heart. Forgiving is highly therapeutic. It heals immensely.

Thank you is the best prayer.

Sometimes you feel gratitude but due to unknown reasons, you hold it. Better express your gratitude and enjoy the benefits. Feeling gratitude and not expressing it is like having a wrapped gift but not giving to the person for whom you brought it. so you don't enjoy the "joy of giving".

Feelings need to be expressed. Well-expressed feelings have great therapeutic effects.

> *"Feel empathy towards others.*
> *Empathy means caring and sharing."*
>
> **—Satessh Singh**

💡 GOLDEN NUGGETS

- *When you take someone's name, they feel that they are respected. They are loved. They are remembered. You care for them*

- *Remember, the sweetest thing to any human being is their name*

- *Human beings love their own name the best. We love to be called by our names*

- *Include three words in your day-to-day life vocabulary (a) Please (b) Excuse me & (c) Thank you*

- *When you are thanking people, be genuine because people can make out whether you are genuine or a fake*

- *A man grows in thier stature when they offer an apology*

- *Feel empathy towards others. Empathy means caring and sharing*

- *When you pardon people, you win their heart. Forgiving is highly therapeutic. It heals immensely*

- *Feelings need to be expressed. Well expressed feelings have great therapeutic effects*

- *The heaviest thing to hold is a grudge*

CHAPTER
Eight

Avoid Arguments and Disagreements

When you argue with someone, you lose a relationship. The reason is when you argue you don't look at their strength areas. You always try to search and find the weaknesses. Believe me, nobody likes to highlight their weaknesses.

The best option is to avoid arguments. Avoid disagreements. Avoid confrontation. Avoid bitterness in your relationship.

Be empathetic to the other person's view. Listen to them carefully. Ask as many questions as possible. You must agree not to disagree.

Remember, every word and expression are available in many languages but the smile is expressed in the same way in all languages. So smile more.

The power of love overshadows the love for power.

Either love or get perished.

We should not argue with someone, instead, we should discuss the topic because discussions are always better than arguments. Argument discontinues relationship whereas discussion helps in building relationships.

Argument is done to find out who is right and discussion is done to find out what is right.

What is critical is what is right and not who is right. But as an ordinary human being, we are always busy finding out who is right and that leads to heartburn.

Say what you feel but never ever say anything which is mean or downgrades somebody.

Let me share one more pleasant experience as a customer when I bought a T-Shirt from a big and famous brand. After the first wash, the T-shirt shrunk. The moment I made a complaint to the outlet manager, I thought they would argue and not agree. To my surprise, they not only agreed and replaced me with another fresh new piece but also their Quality Assurance department wrote me an apology letter with details of the nature of complaint. By agreeing to and addressing my quality complaint, they won a loyal customer forever. A big gain for the brand and company.

When you argue with your customers, you lose them forever. And big brands can't afford to lose their reputation, goodwill and image.

One should behave like a honey bee, always search for the nectar.

Never defeat people in the relationship, instead, try to win them. Happiness doesn't lie in defeating someone, instead, happiness remains in making others win.

> *"A caring heart, sharing ear and fairing mind*
> *is the best quality of a human being."*
>
> **—Satessh Singh**

Remember, silence is very powerful. It is better to lose an argument and win a relationship.

It is said, "Lose the argument but not the person."

Argument is not communication, its noise. Never pollute the atmosphere. Respect the other person. Agree to their point of view. Validate with data and revert back if needed.

When you argue, you create negativity for self and others too. You create a negative reputation and image of both the parties. You don't get any benefits out of an argument.

In fact, research indicates people who argue more have develop more inflammatory-related health issues. So, argumenting not only affects a human being mentally but also physically.

Respect other's opinions by protecting yourself too. The situation can be fragile – hence handle with care.

The best way is to praise people, appreciate people. Be empathetic. Be respectful. Be curious to dig to the bottom of the issue.

Many a times, we hear to reply and not to understand, thereby we miss out many critical pieces of information.

"Better to lose the argument but win a relationship."

—Satessh Singh

💡 GOLDEN NUGGETS

- *When you argue with someone, you lose a relationship*
- *Be empathetic to the other person's view. Listen to them carefully*

- *Every word and expression are available in many languages but the smile is same in all the languages*

- *The power of love overshadows the love for power*

- *Either love or get perished*

- *Argument is done to find out who is right and discussion is done to find out what is right*

- *When you argue with your customer, you lose him forever*

- *One should behave like a honey bee, always search for the nectar*

- *Never defeat people in relationship, instead, try to win them*

- *Better to lose an argument but not the person*

- *Be empathetic and be respectful*

CHAPTER
Nine

Admit Your Mistake with Grace

You must admit your mistake graciously.

I know this could be a difficult task. But still do it and see the magical benefits.

Admission of your own mistake makes you a bigger hero in other persons' eye. People would love and appreciate your courage if you admit your mistakes graciously.

Why people don't admit their mistakes? The answer is, they are scared of social embarrassment and disrespect. They are worried about the consequences. People are scared and worried about losing their reputation. People feel insecure. They carry their mistakes in their heart and mind and keep struggling forever.

The best way is to empty your heart and be light. Feel light. Let me tell you; when you admit your mistake, you feel healed. You feel liberated. It is highly therapeutic.

When we work 365 days and deal with people, we commit mistakes many times knowingly or unknowingly, which is very much pardonable and repairable. But due to social pressure, we carry those mistakes and in the process to hide the mistake, we are forced to commit some more bigger mistakes.

The best remedy is to say 'I admit my mistake and I can repair the same' and keep marching ahead.

One caution here, you can't keep committing the same mistake again and again and keep extending your apologies. No way. If at all committed any mistake then admit your mistake, express your apologies, learn from the mistake and never repeat the same mistake again.

The essence of all virtues is in humility.

Rakesh, who was my Brand Manager, once came to my cabin and admitted that he had made a big blunder and it would cost financial losses to the company. Rakesh was assisting me in one of the companies during my corporate stint. Once he was working on the launch of a division where he was supposed to design a marketing plan. Due to oversight, he and his senior both placed the same order of an input. They came to know about the duplicity of the order only when the stocks arrived. Now, they were shivering about how to handle the situation. But, Rakesh decided to tell the truth. He came to me and with great courage, he admitted his mistake of placing double the quantity of the item. Frankly speaking, I was highly upset but then suddenly I realized what if he would have kept silent? What if he would have kept things under the carpet? What if he and his manager would have started the blame-game? Instead of scolding him, I admired him and encouraged him to always tell truth come what may. I liked the way he admitted his mistakes and got relieved. Later on, we were able to utilize that input for some other Marketing campaign. Thereafter, he never committed that kind of a mistake in his life.

Remember, courage is not the absence of fear but courage is the ability to overcome fear. Be courageous to overcome your fear of admitting your mistakes.

"A man grows in his stature when he offers an apology."

—Satessh Singh

Admitting a mistake always exhibits the power of courage. It takes tons of guts to admit your own mistake the way it takes a lot of guts to forgive someone.

When you admit your mistake, you are free from the guilt. You must have experienced in your past; whenever you had committed a mistake and not admitted, you were always carrying guilt in your heart. When you admit your mistake you are guilt-free. You feel liberated. You enjoy a fearless life.

Once my Super boss (my boss's boss) shouted at me in a meeting without any specific reason. I was wondering why did he scold me? Why did he shout on me? When I replayed the entire episode in my mind to find out the trigger point, I couldn't find the logic why did he had raised his voice. By the end of the meeting, I expressed my surprise and unhappiness to him in a very polite but firm manner and left the meeting point. Same day around 9.30 pm, I got several texts from the same boss stating " I am extremely sorry to lose my temperament. I could have avoided that episode which was uncalled for. Normally, I don't behave the way I behaved with you today during the meeting. Please accept my sincere apology and excuse me.

I would feel better and light if you can accept my invitation to have a cup of coffee tomorrow in the corporate coffee shop." You know, I was badly hurt and disturbed by his behavior during the meeting. I was highly agitated and was mentally disturbed. But when I got his text, I could sense that he was very genuine in his expression and was truly a deserving person to be forgiven from my end. I moved on after replying, " Please handle your emotions more carefully in the future so that you don't have to be sorry next time." I was totally relieved and relaxed. I admired his courage to be apologetic and for the courage to admit his mistake. He deserved a new chance and we became a great team in the coming days. Very soon I was his blue-eyed executive.

When you say sorry to someone, it is a sign that you care and respect for the other person. This could be a great foundation for a solid relationship. You value more of your human values and less of your ego.

When you extend your apology, you get to earn genuine love and admiration when the other person realizes how courageous it was of you to say sorry.

There are times when by admitting your mistake you can save your relationships. This can go a long way in maintaining your healthy relationships with your family, friends, relatives and business clients.

When you say sorry, the other person feels you are a humble man. They feel you are a genuine human being.

They get a feeling that you are not an arrogant man. They believe in your genuine approach, attitude and sincere attempt to improve your relationship and that makes you a true gentleman.

 ## GOLDEN NUGGETS ──────────────────────────

- *You must admit your mistake graciously*

- *Empty your heart and be light. Feel liberated*

- *The essence of all virtues is in humility*

- *Courage is not the absence of fear but courage is the ability to overcome fear. Be courageous to overcome your fear of admitting your mistakes*

- *Admitting a mistake always exhibits the power of courage*

- *When you say sorry to someone, it is a sign that you care and respect for the other person. This could be a great foundation for a solid relationship*

- *hen you say sorry, the other person feels you are a humble man.*

CHAPTER
Ten

Appreciate People and Avoid Complaints

When was the last time you appreciated yourself? Don't remember! That's a very common mistake we make as a human being. Sometimes we are too tight in judging ourselves. We over reprimand ourselves. We don't give the benefit of doubt to self. Let us not treat ourselves too brutally.

Charity must begin from home.

Hence, today take out some time and first appreciate yourself. You must appreciate yourself for all the good things you have done to yourself, your family, your friends, your relatives, your colleagues and customers.

Always meet and greet people with a smiley and cheerful face. Show warmth and affection in your body language.

Be appreciative about the other person. Admire the other persons' positive things to connect with them. Start your conversation by calling them by their name. As mentioned earlier, every human being likes to be called by their name. First-thing-first talk good about them. Be honest, genuine and authentic. If you try to be fake, you would be caught.

Find many ways to say that you care about them. Include some of the appreciative sentences like: "I like your dressing sense" "I like the way you think and speak" " I enjoy spending time with you" "I really appreciate for your valuable inputs" "You are one of my best friends whom I can trust and rely". These are magical statements which will make you a hero in the eyes of the other person.

Once I invited Mr. Surendra Prasad, a 60-year-old and highly energetic corporate world veteran who retired from a topmost corporate. Now he is a Director Placement in one of the reputed universities. So, he was my guest and also one among the three panelists who came to judge the team of participants who were competing in a corporate excellence program. The event started right from 9 am onwards and went on till late evening. I was amused to see his energy and enthusiasm till the end of the day. Besides, not even once he made any complaint about anything. In fact, the whole day he was praising and encouraging each and every participant to give their best and finally all the participants were highly influenced by his great influential personality. He liked the entire process and participants. Even the participants liked him as a jury. He was only and only praising people and infusing energy among them.

"Negativity dehydrates but positivity rehydrates."

—Satessh Singh

You must accept people as they are. Never ever try to find faults in them. Never try to make them feel low. Instead, you must boost their morale as and when they need it. Read them carefully. Be empathetic to them. Sponsor them. Absorb their shortcomings and help them to become strong and stronger.

You must compliment them for all their small and big achievements, knowledge, skills and personality.

Remember, all human beings love to be appreciated. In fact, people who are appreciated and motivated are better achievers in their life.

"When we replace expectation with appreciation,
we enjoy utmost satisfaction."

—Satessh Singh

Remember, your appreciation can change many lives forever. When you appreciate, you infuse a tremendous amount of confidence and faith in the other person. If you don't show appreciation to the other person that they deserve then they may not come up to your expectations. Because an appreciated person always tries to outperform.

Keep giving the booster dose of appreciation and create an aura of a highly appreciative world.

You need to produce positive energy in and around you. Keep spreading positivity in your surroundings.

Keep in mind, what you send outside would return back to you. If you send appreciation to others, the Universe would appreciate you too.

"Be passionate about your relationships."

💡 GOLDEN NUGGETS

- *Always meet and greet people with a smiley and cheerful face. Show warmth and affection in your body language*

- *Negativity dehydrates but positivity rehydrates*

- *You must accept people as they are*

- *You must compliment them for all their small and big achievements, knowledge, skills and personality*

- *All human beings love to be appreciated*

- *Your appreciation can change someone's life*

- *Keep giving booster dose of appreciation and create an aura of highly appreciative world*

- *You need to produce positive energy in and around you*

- *Keep in mind, what you send outside would return back to you*

CHAPTER
Eleven

Have Patience

Patience is your ability to wait for something without getting irritated. Having patience means you can remain calm even when you have been waiting for something or someone.

Patience is a gift to humanity. It is a capacity to accept anything easily without feeling much bad about it. A person with the power of patience can tackle any difficulty in his life without getting angry and irritated.

Patience is an important tool for overcoming frustration.

HDFC Bank is a reputed bank with a team of like-minded professionals. Once I saw a customer getting impatient and arguing with the manager Dipali Pawar, who happens to be the most dynamic executive of the branch. She was trying her best to convince the customer about what needs to be done in a prescribed manner as per the bank's rules and regulations. But the customer was not at all ready to listen to her and got hyper which all other customers also felt was unwanted. Finally, Dipali said if you are not ready to listen then how would I resolve your problem? Instead of listening to her suggestions, he was shouting, screaming and parading his anger and arrogance. Dipali made her best efforts to convince him which took a lot of time. Finally, when the customer agreed to listen to her then he realized the mistake was on his part and not the bank's. However, Dipali helped him to resolve his problem not only despite her wasted time and efforts but she had also been hurt by the customer's impatient behavior.

You got to practice patience to get rid of your own anxiety and frustration.

Look at things as per other persons' perspective. Do justice to the opposite person's views and situations. Don't be too judgemental. Don't be too pushy.

Nobody wants to delay things. Sometimes the situation is beyond control and sometimes people practice procrastination, thereby, things get delayed. If the situation is responsible then give the benefit of doubt to other person and if they are delaying it deliberately then have a simple and humble dialogue to understand the real cause.

Do the root-cause analysis. Patience is not the ability to wait but it is how you act, react and respond while you are waiting.

Don't be reactive. Be responsive. Don't carry fixed ideas about the other person or the situation. Wait for some time. Give the benefit of doubt to the other person as you expect for yourself.

Patience reflects your maturity to deal with any situation. Patience also indicates your wisdom. Patience is the companion of wisdom.

Give your decent time and reasonable patience to the other person. Allow them to explain to you their situation or difficulty.

Patience and silence are two powerful energies. Patience makes you mentally strong and silence makes you emotionally strong.

Before reacting to anybody or any situation, step in the other person's shoes. Be practical. Be realistic. Be original.

Don't judge people from the lens of one episode. Don't write off anybody on the basis of one mistake. Have patience and wait till the climax. It is like a 6 and 9. You may be able to see a 6 but the other person is seeing it as a 9. Neither of you are wrong. It's a matter of wearing each other's shoes and understanding what is right and not who is right.

"Patience and silence are two powerful energies."

 ## GOLDEN NUGGETS

- *Patience is a gift to humanity*

- *Patience is an important tool for overcoming frustration*

- *You ought to practice patience to get rid of your own anxiety and frustration*

- *Look at things as per other person's perspective*

- *Patience is not the ability to wait but how you act, react and respond while you are waiting*

- *Don't be reactive. Be responsive*

- *Patience reflects your maturity to deal with any situation*

- *Patience is the companion of wisdom*

- *Patience and silence are two powerful energies. Patience makes you mentally strong and silence makes you emotionally strong*

- *Don't judge people from the lens of one episode*

- *Don't write off anybody just because of one mistake*

- *Give the benefit of doubt to others*

CHAPTER *Twelve*

Leave an Everlasting Impression

The first impression is the everlasting impression.

You must have experienced many times; you like somebody in the first meeting only - for no reason. Similarly, you may not like somebody when you meet them for no reason. This is a natural frequency and affinity to each other.

Many times you leave a mark in the first impression only. You achieve this by showing your warmth, your seriousness in the other person, your honesty and sincerity while talking to the person.

What leaves a mark is your preparation on a particular topic or meeting. Your punctuality. Your positivity. Your positive body language. Your honest admission of the mistakes. Your nature and habit of forgiving other person's mistakes.

You can leave an lasting impression by allowing the other person to speak more. Through your active listening. By maintaining your eye-to-eye contact while talking. By using some of the magical statements like " Please" " Thank you" "Apology" "Sorry" "I like your company" " I love your personality" " I appreciate your suggestions" "I admire your knowledge and skills". When you use these statements during your interaction, you are bound to leave a mark on the other person.

You win the heart and mind of the person.

Always try to give importance to the other person. Make the other person feel like a VIP.

Energize the other person with your listening ability. Infuse confidence in he other person. Respect their views. Don't judge. Have patience.

Don't react but respond.

Ask clarifications on the subject which you don't know or don't understand. Be courageous to admit your mistake. Seek advice. Take opinion.

Don't take any criticism personally. Neither criticize anybody. Be supportive. Accept people as they are. Be thankful. Be courteous.

Harsh Mariwalla is the Founder Chairman of Marico Industries who owns brands like Parachute oil, Saffola to name a few. In one of the corporate events, he was invited to share his wisdom on the topic "INNOVATION". Innovation is his favorite topic on which he always loves to share his wisdom. I could see a lot of passion in his talk when he was delivering his insight on innovation. I also participated in that event. I asked him many rational and irrational questions which not only he replied patiently but during the tea breaks, he came to me and appreciated some of my inquisitive questions. He praised me and motivated me by his aura. I could feel an everlasting impact of his personality that day onwards.

He left a great influence on me. I carry a very high image and respect for Harsh Mariwalla.

It is said, **"You don't get a second chance to make a great FIRST impression."**

Hence, the first impression must be an everlasting impression.

The way you present yourself is the way people first view you.

Elliott Abrams said beautifully "First impressions matter. Experts say we size up new people in somewhere between 30 seconds to 2 minutes."

J.K.Rowling said, "A good first impression can work wonders." How true she is.

We keep many good or bad experiences of our first meeting and first interaction.

Either we leave an impression or we bring an impression whenever we meet somebody for the first time.

When we leave an impression, we become a charismatic and magnetic personality. People are attracted to us. People love to be around us. People like our company. We are at the center stage of the personality.

"Choose words that make the heart soar and not sore."

—Satessh Singh

 **GOLDEN NUGGETS** ───────────────

- *First impression is everlasting impression*
- *Always try to give importance to the other person. Make the other person feel like a VIP*

- *Energize the other person with your listening ability*

- *Ask clarifications on the subject which you don't know or don't understand*

- *Be courageous to admit your mistake. Seek advice. Take opinion*

- *Don't take any criticism personally. Neither criticize anybody. Be supportive.*

- *You don't get a second chance to make a great FIRST impression*

- *How you present yourself is how people first view you*

- *Either we leave an impression or we bring an impression whenever we meet some body for the first time*

CHAPTER
Thirteen

Dress to be Addressed

Dress how you want to be addressed.

Dressing is significant not only in the sense of your attire but also in the overall outlook. Dressing up as per the occasion is always an ideal situation but attire is only one part of the dress code.

You should also have an overall impactful dressing to suit the occasion. One should read the occasion and event and dress accordingly.

Be formal in formal forums and informal in informal events. Don't do it either way.

Wear a smile on the face. Be cheerful. Be energetic. Be live. Be graceful. Show warmth. Be impactful. Let the other person mirror you. Let the other person get positively influenced by your dressing sense. Let him upgrade.

Create energy in the atmosphere through your dress code. Look classy and not clumsy. Keep in mind the climate, environment, season and occasion while finalizing your dressing style. Ask and get it clear about the dress code on a particular occasion.

The part of looking classy is having good posture. Always keep a straight back, look in front of you instead of at the ground and avoid slouching as much as you can. Don't cross your arms over your chest but keep them at your sides to help your chest open up. If you lift your head high, you will look and feel more classy.

In short, have a power-dressing sense because appearance is very much important to create a positive impression.

When you dress shabbily, people remember the dress but when you dress impeccably, people remember you. When you dress like everybody else then you don't have to think like everybody else.

You will never find something to wear that makes you feel beautiful, smart or loved if you don't believe that you already are.

Clothing should be a form of self-expression. Dressing gives an indication and hint of who you are.

Fashion is what you buy but style is what you do with it. Always dress well, keep it simple but significant.

Dressing elegantly means your personality and appearance match and complement each other.

Devendra Jha is an Executive in a private bank in Mumbai city. A very humble and a middle-class young man from a small town of Bihar near Patna city. He is a graduate, an MBA and a highly aspirational young man. I met him in his branch to open up my savings account. At first sight, I was highly impressed to see his dressing sense. He was a well-groomed and well-dressed man. He has two different ways of dressing up himself. When he is in office, he is very professionally and formally dressed up. He also has a few friends who are connected to Bollywood and he likes to visit Bollywood celebrity parties and other page-three parties with his friends. He meets and greets all celebrities and clicks pics and selfies with them. But when I saw his celebrity night or page-three pics, I was totally bowled out. For a moment I couldn't realize and recognize that he was Devendra Jha a middle-class junior bank executive. He was looking absolutely stunning. He was looking like a celebrity. He was carrying the high positive impact of Power Dressing. Kudos to Devendra Jha and his sense of power dressing.

 ## GOLDEN NUGGETS

- *Dress how you want to be addressed*

- *Be formal in formal forums and informal in informal events. Don't do it either way*

- *Create energy in the atmosphere through your dress code*

- *Clothing should be a form of self-expression. Dressing gives an indication and hint of who you are*

- *Fashion is what you buy but style is what you do with it*

- *Your dressing sense must be appreciated by other people*

- *Dressing elegantly means your personality and appearance match and complement each other*

CHAPTER
Fourteen

Keep Safe Distance from Negative People

Keep a safe distance from negative people. Such people are talented enough to transfer their negativity to you. They have the ability to infect you. Their negativity is contagious. Their negativity is highly spreadable. They can ruin your growth.

If you want to be financially rich then be in the company of financially rich people but if you want to become intellectually rich then do friendship with intellectually rich people.

It is said that we are an average of five people surrounding us. You can check yourself. Just find out your best 5 friends or relatives or colleagues who are closely connected to you. These are the people you are regularly interacting and spending maximum time with. Now you can find out from them their average annual income and calculate the same. You would be surprised to know that your income would be the same or similar to their average incomes. Similar is the case of intellectual level and mental status.

Now, what if you are having 5 negative mindset people in your inner circle? Obviously, you would be developing and acquiring their negative mindset. Therefore, the best way is to keep a safe distance without their knowledge that you are maintaining distance from them.

Either you influence your surroundings positively or avoid getting influenced negatively.

Did you notice anytime when you listen to some slow or sad song, your energy goes down drastically? Similarly, when you listen to some fast track or a peppy song, you become highly energetic.

This is the reason why in the ancient India, familyhead or grandparents used to tell a motivational story or mythological story to the young family members, especially children, to infuse great culture in them. Either in the early morning or evening, there used to be a satsang (storytelling sessions) which used to purify people's mind and they used to help people and society to adopt and build great human values.

Nowadays, our new society is missing all those great storytelling sessions.

My grandfather used to tell me at least one mythological or spiritual or family-related story when I was a child. I learnt many insights related to Ramayana, Mahabharta, Bhagwadgita, Quran and great Indian warriors like Shivaji Maharaj, Maha Rana Pratap, Bhagat Singh, Chandrashekhar Azad, Tipu Sultan and many such great Indians through his storytelling. That was the power of storytelling.

If you are not inspired about your own legacy then very soon your legacy would get expired. Very soon your values will get vanished. Very soon you would lose the edge. You would lose your energy. You would have no zeal for life. No life thereafter. Absolutely extinct personality.

How often do you come across a person who doesn't have energy; who doesn't have life? They are absolutely dull and lethargic. Full of negativity and pessimism.

"Keep a safe distance from negative people."

—Satessh Singh

If you don't keep a safe distance from such people, they would make you the way they are.

If you can't influence somebody positively then refrain yourself from getting influenced by their negatively. Keep a safe distance from such people.

GOLDEN NUGGETS

- *Keep a safe distance from negative people*

- *If you want to be financially rich then be in company of financially rich people and if you want to become intellectually rich then do friendship with intellectually rich people*

- *If you can't influence somebody positively then refrain from getting influenced negatively*

CHAPTER
Fifteen

Forgive, Forget and Ignore

If you can't forgive someone then forget them. If you can't forget their mistakes then ignore their mistake.

"Never try to defeat people, instead try to win them."

—Satessh Singh

When you try to defeat people, you are tempted to go unethical. When you hurt people, you create a distance between both; you and the person. People start going against you. But when you try to win people, respect their space, respect their privacy, respect their situation, respect their circumstances; finally you win their heart.

You can't hurt somebody. You are not privileged to damage anyone's self-esteem and pride. Don't push too much. Leave it. Let the time take its own course. Allow others to save their face. Allow them to bounce back with great pride and esteem.

If forgiveness becomes difficult then forget the episode and erase that memory. Press shift and delete button and remove it from your hard disc. Empty your mind and heart. Do sanitize your heart. Wipeout with some holy thoughts and move on. Life is action, keep going and keep moving ahead.

Don't be too personal. Don't store that memory in your hard disc forever. Refresh your recycle bin. Give benefit of doubt to the other person.

Still, if you find the other person is not coming up to your expectations then don't lower down your expectations, instead, start pulling up the person by offering a helping hand. Ignore events and not the person.

The same people behave differently in a different environment.

Devendra Sharma was a Product Manager in a pharma company where I joined as his manager. He was very close to the BU Head and was in the system for the last 2 years. He was also aspiring to get elevated but after gauging his capabilities, the BU Head preferred to hire me instead of promoting him. I started with flying colours just within a week's time. The BU Head was highly impressed by my work. However, to my surprise, after 8 days I was told by the HR Manager that I was not required so I won't get that job. I couldn't understand what went wrong. After some time, I came to know that Devendra Sharma was jealous of me and he infected the BU Head against me. Both of them played dirty politics and within 8 days, I became a jobless man. I remained jobless for almost six months; it was tough time for me and my family since meeting the expenses had turned into an uphill battle.

Now, twist in the story. After 10 years, same Devendra Sharma came for an interview when I was a BU Head. He had applied for the post of Head Marketing. Now the destiny played a different game with him. The moment he entered my cabin for his interview we both recognized each other. He found it quite embarrassing to face me but

I showed that I didn't know what he had done with me . I selected him and supported him to become a high flier. Now, he is a General Manager in an MNC.

Here, in this case, I tried to win him and not defeat him. Today, he is a big fan of mine and a changed person too. Hope he reads this chapter and realizes how his mindset to defeat me made me a bigger hero. We should try to win people and not defeat people.

Winning gives positivity and defeating gives negativity.

 **GOLDEN NUGGETS** ————————————

- *If you can't forgive someone then forget him. If you can't forget someone then ignore their mistakes*

- *Never try to defeat people instead try to win them*

- *Give benefit of doubt to the other person*

- *The same person behaves differently in a different environment and situation*

CHAPTER
Sixteen

Become a Buyer

Become a buyer and not a seller!

Generally, you try to sell your point. You try to sell your concept. In that process, you get trapped in a situation where knowingly or unknowingly, you start arguing with the other person and you lose them.

When you argue with someone, you lose a relationship.

What is important? Winning an argument and losing a relationship or losing an argument but winning a relationship? Obviously the latter one.

You need to buy the other person's point. Don't criticize, instead, be inquisitive. Seek clarity. Ask for opinion. Ask for the evidence, ask for the data. Get convinced and buy his point.

Become a buyer. A buyer always asks for more and more details about a product or aservice. A buyer always looks for value. A buyer has all the right to get convinced before buying a point, product or service.

Remember, the buyer is the king. So be a buyer.

Don't push too hard to sell your point beyond a limit. It's not worth. Leave it after some point. When you try to sell too hard, it won't get sold. If the sale doesn't happen in the first 2 minutes, it won't happen in two hours or two days or two weeks.

Yes, when you buy a point the other person is open to discuss and listen to you.

I would suggest; never sell your point. Instead, buy other's point. Win their heart and become a superstar.

"Happiness is not a pleasure; it's a victory."

—Satessh Singh

When you buy the other person's point he is sold to you. You are a winner.

Always first buy and agree to the other's point and then say "In addition to what you said, I would like to add something which may add value to your point." I am sure the other person will like this technique because you have already won him by buying and agreeing to his point.

Remember: Buyer is a king. Remain a king forever.

💡 GOLDEN NUGGETS

- *Become a buyer and not a seller*
- *Don't criticize instead be enquisitive. Be curious*
- *Buyer is a king*
- *When you buy a point, then the other person is open to discus and listen to you*
- *Happiness is not a pleasure; it's a victory*
- *When you buy the other persons point, he is sold to you.*

CHAPTER
Seventeen

Be a Trust-Booster and not Trust-Buster

The word trust is highly important in our day-to-day life to become an influential personality.

The word TRUST itself describes its value and impact beautifully.

Let us look at the word. When you remove the alphabet 'T' from the word Trust, it becomes 'RUST'. It loses its value and impact completely. From a thing of great power it becomes an unwanted phenomena.

Hence, you need to become a 'Trust-booster' and not a 'Trust-buster'.

Any two individuals can develop a tremendous amount of trust between them by being a consistent and persistent partner to each other. Their repetitive actions, responses, consistency, persistency and timely reciprocation without a reminder would boost the trust level.

When we give commitment, we give hope and when we live up to the commitment, we fulfill the hope and then Trust is developed. Fulfillment of hope is the key to build trust. People love to deal with those who are trustworthy. People are scared of insecurity. They need security and commitments. They need to be comfortable and feel secure.

"A commitment gives hope. A fulfilled hope is called trust."

—Satessh Singh

Whether a friendship, relationship, partnership or a buyer and seller relationship; every bond is built on trust. If there is a dearth of trust then no relationships can be built.

"I trust you" is a better compliment than "I love you" because you may not always trust a person you love but you can always love a person whom you trust.

Trust is built over a period of time. Trust requires a track record. Trust requires consistency. Trust requires some critical sacrifices. Trust requires to shed off the ego. Trust is tested in a tough and difficult time.

As a consumer, when we decide to buy any FMCG product, we check the ratings and trust the index of a product or its manufacturer. We come across many reputed brands which have a very high trust index. We are always guaranteed to get the value for our money after buying the same.

Management Guru Philip Kotler beautifully said, ***"The best advertising is done by a satisfied customer."***

Now, who is a satisfied customer? A customer neither buys a product nor a service. They buy a 'solution' to their 'problem'. We can't offer them a problem against their earlier problem. It's annoying and disgusting. It is a trust-buster. We need to offer a solution instead.

Similarly, when you have a long track record of trust then people would become your 'Brand Ambassador'. If you don't have a track record of trust then it would be a herculean task to develop and build trust for you. You fail to become a brand. You are just a commodity.

One thing to keep in mind - you should never break the commitment and trust.

Tata group, Mahindra group and Birla group command a very high degree of trust among their customers in India. Infosys, Apple, Microsoft and Wipro are some examples of a very high level of trust index. That's why they enjoy the premium customer loyalty. They have a huge and endless list of satisfied customers.

In personal branding also, trust plays a vital role to build an individual image. People refer to those who have a very high personal brand equity. People who command a very high trust index are the most loved and appreciated. People who have a very high trust index command premiums.

🔦 GOLDEN NUGGETS

- *You need to become a Trust-Booster and not a trust-buster*

- *When we give commitment, we give hope and when we live up to the commitment, we fulfil the hope and that becomes Trust*

- *Whether its friendship or relationship, every bond is built on trust. No trust no relationship*

- *Trust requires a track record. Trust requires a legacy*

- *The best advertising is done by a satisfied customer*

- *People who have a very high trust index command premiums*

CHAPTER
Eighteen
Acquire P.A.I.S.A

Do you have P.A.I.S.A? Do you wish to earn P.A.I.S.A?

The P.A.I.S.A is a highly critical and life-changing formula. If you study about all the great achievers of the Universe, you would find that they all have had a great amount of P.A.I.S.A.

Now, let's learn what P.A.I.S.A is.

P stands for Passion, A stands for Aspiration, I stands for Inspiration, S stands for Satisfaction and A stands for Aggression.

If you look at any successful person whether in the field of science, business, education, politics, sports, Hollywood, Bollywood etc, you would find they possess an abundance of P.A.I.S.A. in them. Higher the P.A.I.S.A; higher the success.

Passion is defined as a strong feeling of enthusiasm or excitement for something or about doing something. Passion instills madness in a person to do something in a highly extraordinary manner to impact our society positively.

Sachin Tendulkar is a classic example of the word 'passion'. In one of the interviews, his roommate and batchmate Vinod Kambli mentioned that Sachin used to wake up in the night and practice with his kit to bring accuracy and edge to his batting technique. He was mad behind enhancing his batting abilities. He was consistent and crazy.

Amitabh Bachchan is another legend who has a very high passion for his work i.e. acting. In a book called 'Pandeymonium' the Ad Guru Piyush Pandey mentioned that after every shot Amitabh would come and ask his director if he is satisfied by his shot or not. In case the Director shows even a small indication of compromise which Amitabh can make out from his/her body language then he would go for a retake. It has been more than half a century of his acting experience and he is one of the finest actors in India but he still follows his director's guidelines. This is called passion.

Steve Jobs was another huge practitioner of the word Passion. He was highly passionate about his design. He was a true genius and highly passionate about the Apple products. He once said, "We're here to put a dent in the universe. Otherwise, why else even be here?" What a way to look at himself and his business. A great gift to mankind who disrupted the entire world of communication.

The word **Aspiration** is defined as a strong desire or ambition to achieve something. Aspiration is a strong hope, dream or goal. The idea of aspiration has a positive and upward connotation.

Music director and singer Shankar Mahadevan always had an aspiration to become a singer and musician despite his engineering degree. Finally, he achieved what he aspired to become. Same is the case with actor Madhavan who is a qualified engineer but aspired to become an actor. Cricketers like Srinath and K Srikanth were engineers too but became highly successful cricketers. The entire credit goes to their aspiration to become what they aspired to be.

Inspiration is defined as the process of being mentally stimulated to do something. Inspire means to excite, encourage or breathe life into something. Being an inspiration means being the force or influence that inspires someone to do something great.

Inspiration is an intrinsic factor. Inspiration is self-charging. It is highly purposeful. I got inspired to write this book and share all my wisdom with my readers. Nobody pushed me or pulled me to write. I strongly believe knowledge and wisdom increase manifold when it is shared with many people. When a person gets inspired, he achieves something extraordinary in his life. He does something which is out of the world.

Satisfaction is defined as an act of fulfillment and contentment. Satisfaction is a pleasant or positive emotion. It can also be a feeling. It can even be a state of mind.

> *"Human being always lives in a tent,*
> *either content or discontent."*
>
> **—Satessh Singh**

Bill Gates - Microsoft, Azim Premjee - Wipro, Warren Buffet - Hathway, Vineet Nayar - HCL, Narayan Murthy - Infosys, Dr. Devi Shetty - Narayana Hrudalaya and umpteen such personalities are the live examples of great people who are highly satisfied by contributing towards society.

Aggression means a person who makes a strong attempt to win. A man who gives his everything to achieve something great in his life which can have a great positive impact.

Virat Kohli is one such aggressive cricketer who plays very dynamically to win the matches. After he steps in the field, he gives his best to bring glory to his country.

People who possess limitless P.A.I.S.A. in their life are the ones who write history. They create many success stories. They impact society. They leave a legacy. They become immortal and unforgettable.

One who gives his best; gets the best.

💡 GOLDEN NUGGETS ────────────────

- *P stands for PASSION, A stands for Aspiration, I stands for Inspiration, S stands for Satisfaction and A stands for Aggression*

- *Passion instills madness in a person to do something in a highly extra ordinary manner*

- *Aspiration is defined as a strong desire or ambition to achieve something*

- *Inspiration means to excite, encourage or breathe life into.*

- *Inspiration is an intrinsic factor. Inspiration is self-charging. It is highly purposeful*

- *Satisfaction is a pleasant or positive emotion. The best advertising is done by a satisfied customer*

- *Aggression means a person who makes a strong attempt to win. A man who gives his everything to achieve something great in his life*

CHAPTER
Nineteen

Leaders are Readers

This is very true that all the leaders are great readers.

After completing your graduation and post–graduation, now you must be in a corporate, semi-government, State Govt., Central government, MNC company or working oversees and enjoying your professional life.

Then what is the need for you to read now? Very logical question. Let me tell you, once we leave university, we hardly get an opportunity to go back and refresh our learnings in those universities. Then what is the other way out to upgrade ourselves?

Books are the only and most affordable source to upgrade our knowledge.

"People who are not updated are outdated."

—Satessh Singh

The way our smartphone needs to upgrade and update its software, similarly we need to upgrade and update our mental software.

I agree and am aware that many people don't love and like to read the book, hence they spend more time in front of their TV sets. If TV enhances our knowledge and adds value to our skills then we must watch it. If you are watching for the sake of entertainment then have a limited dose. Don't be addicted.

Majority of people use Facebook but they hardly make efforts to put their face into a book. I am not against any social media platforms. They are powerful tools to gain knowledge, skills and upgrade oneself but reading a book is like reading an author's mind, reading his ideology, reading his concepts and creativities. Even if you apply one idea out of those books into your life, you can change your future and fortune forever.

I can suggest you a very innovative method of reading a book. Initially, start buying a thin and slim book of not more than 100 or 125 pages. Develop a habit of reading 5 pages a day which will take maximum of 10-15 minutes. Once you develop the liking for reading a book, you can buy a book of 150 to 200 pages.

I read 5-6 books in a month, so yearly I read at least 50 to 60 books. I read when I am travelling. I get enough time to do so.

I can also suggest another interesting way of reading a book. While reading a book, you can use highlighters of different colours. Whichever sentence you find worth and special that add value in your life, you highlight them. If you like several sentences on the same page then you can use a different coloured highlighter so that it stands out. Now once you complete the first read and in future whenever you need to refer to those books or sentences, you need not re-read the entire book, instead, you can just go through those highlighted sentences. It saves your time and makes reading more interesting. Why don't you try this innovative technique of reading a book?

Highlight what you like. Highlight the highly impactful sentences.

When you read a book, you come to know how different people sitting in different cities or countries are thinking and looking at things in a different way. Just by reading a book by an author from a different country like US, UK, Canada and cities like Delhi, Mumbai, Kolkata, Chennai, Hyderabad, Bengaluru or any other; you can read the author's mind.

What a strong and effective media to acquire knowledge and skills through reading a book! It's a great tool to look at things in a different perspective. This really broadens out your mindset.

The great scientist and former President of India Dr. APJ Kalam wrote: "The day you complete 50 books you would become a great man." That's the power of book reading.

Readers can become great leaders. A great human being. A highly successful man.

Today, you must commit to yourself that here onwards you must read at least one book every month.

Remember, self-commitment can't be broken. Therefore, once you commit to yourself, you must ensure you fulfil.

I would love to mention the names of some of the very powerful self-help books at the end of this book so that you can pick and choose and read them. Read books written by Swami Vivekananda, Mahatma Gandhi, Dale Carnegie, Napoleon Hill, Wayne Dyer, Brian Tracy, Norman Vincent Peale, James Allen, Malcolm Gladwell, Spencer Johnson, Rhonda Byrne, Robert Kiyosaki, Robert Schuller, Tony Robbins, Paulo Coelho, Eckhart Tolle, Deepak Chopra, David J.Schwartz and Robin Sharma to name a few great authors who have written life-changing books. Their books have changed the life of millions, so they can change yours too.

When you learn and apply your learnings, your scope to become a highly successful individual increases many folds.

So, folks, enjoy reading.

I can guarantee, you will invent a new and highly powerful self.

"The readers can become great leaders."

—Satessh Singh

 **GOLDEN NUGGETS** ———————————————

- *All leaders are great readers*

- *People who are not updated are out-dated*

- *Books are the most affordable media to upgrade your knowledge*

- *Even if you apply one idea into your real life, you can change your future and fortune*

- *Develop a habit of reading 5 pages in a day which will take maximum 10-15 minutes*

- *Highlight what you like*

- *Readers can become a great leader. A great human being. A highly successful man*

- *When you learn and apply your learnings, your scope to become a highly successful individual increases many folds*

CHAPTER
Twenty

Applied Knowledge is the Real Power

I read and hear at many places and many times that knowledge is power.

How true is it? Let's scratch our head and understand the whole concept of knowledge.

For example, you have the knowledge on how to drive a car or a motorbike but you don't drive when you are required to drive? You are driving on a highway but you don't apply the brake at the time of the need and crash the car into another vehicle which could have been easily avoided by applying the brake timely.

Can we say in the above case that knowledge is power? Of course not. In the current era of internet, knowledge is available in abundance. What is more important is that you need to apply your right knowledge at the right time for the right purpose.

Hence, "applied knowledge is the real power".

I loved the old corporate logo of Wipro "Applying thoughts"; what a deep meaning! When one applies the thought, the outcome is totally extraordinary.

Now let me recite a very famous story you all might have heard. But I would love to share it again here. A factory, which was running round the clock, was highly profitable where machines were producing some extraordinary stuff. Once something went wrong in one of the machines and the production was stopped, thereby, affecting productivity. Everybody was worried in the factory to restore the machine and therefore they invited many technocrats and engineers to fix the fault so that production can be restored. Unfortunately, all the experts failed to detect the cause of the malfunction. Somebody suggested to call an old man who lived on the outskirts of the city. Since there was no other option, this old man was called. He looked at the machine for some time and asked for a hammer. At one particular point, he banged the hammer and asked the operator to start the machine. Surprisingly, the machine started working and all were happy and delighted as the production was restored. After a few days, the company received a bill of two lakhs from the old man. The CFO asked for the break-up with details of the bill, stating that the charges were too high. The old man sent a revised bill and mentioned (a) for repairing the charges are just ten thousand (b) knowledge and expertise of where to hit the hammer the charges are one lac ninety thousand.

This story conveys that only knowledge is not enough, instead, how to apply that knowledge is more critical. Applied knowledge is the real power.

Therefore, you should acquire new knowledge and apply that to become powerful, productive and an achiever.

Knowledge, if not applied, is just a piece of information and today only information doesn't have any value. Today, an abundance of knowledge is available on social media.

But only when it's applied does it bring success and adds up to your wisdom.

Many times, we learn a new skill but we don't apply. We don't utilize. We don't optimize. The reason could be the fear of starting, the fear of failure, the fear of peer, and fear of what others will say if you don't do well. We prefer to practice procrastination.

The best way to become a champion is to start and keep evolving, keep improving. Follow the concept of kaizen. There's nothing called perfection. Perfection is an illusion. Start early and end early. During the journey, you can keep evolving, keep improving and keep becoming a champion of champions.

Don't wait for perfection else you won't start and will miss the ship.

"Knowledge, when applied, gives wisdom."

—Satessh Singh

Keep acquiring and upgrading your knowledge and become a champion of champions by applying the same. Don't hesitate. Don't feel shy. Go ahead and grab it.

Knowledge belongs to you and when you apply it, the benefit will come to you. Don't look at what the world will say. Keep applying and then see what the world says after some time when you are a highly successful person. The world will salute you when you add value to society.

The world belongs only to the achievers. History belongs to those who create something extraordinary. The world recognizes those who impact the life of millions.

Remember, achievement comes from the application of the knowledge. Keep learning and keep earning. Learning gives the opportunity to grow in life and enhance your earning too. Earning is a by-product of knowledge application.

Look at the powerful spelling of the word 'learning'. Learning is a very inspiring word. First alphabet L then earning, hence keep learning, keep applying and keep earning. When you apply your learnings, you are bound to get success.

 **GOLDEN NUGGETS** ———————————

- *Applied knowledge is the real power*

- *You should acquire new knowledge and skill and apply the same to become a productive and successful man*

- *Knowledge, if not applied, is just an information*

- *Knowledge, when applied, brings success and adds up to wisdom*

- *Develop a habit of reading 5 pages in a day which will take a maximum 10-15 minutes*

- *The best way to become a champion is to start immediately and keep evolving, keep improving*

- *There's nothing called perfection. Perfection is an illusion*

- *Start early and end early*

- *During the journey keep evolving, keep improving and keep becoming a champion of the champion*

- *Knowledge, when applied, becomes wisdom*

- *History belongs to those who create something extraordinary*

- *World recognizes those who impact the life of millions*

CHAPTER
Twenty One

Wish People on their Special Occasions

Every human being likes to be given importance. We love to be noticed, recognized and feel important when somebody treats us like a VIP.

When somebody wishes you on your special occasions like birthdays or wedding anniversaries, you feel delighted. Similarly, others also feel happy and delighted when you wish them on their special occasions.

Check if you have the birth anniversary or wedding anniversary dates of your family members, friends, relatives, peers, superiors and juniors in your office, team members, vendors and customers. If no then please start collecting and maintaining in your smartphone which is smart enough to bring into your notice as and when the occasion arrives.

I have been doing it for the last twenty years. I have a data bank of almost two thousand plus people who were or who are close to me. I even maintain a record of birthdays and wedding anniversary dates of people whom I haven't met in person for the last twenty years but we connected through somebody.

I make it a point to wish them by dropping a text message or I call and wish them personally on their special occasions. So even if I have a list of two thousand plus people, on an average, I wish five to six people every day which is humanly possible.

I dedicate a few minutes daily to wish them and make people feel like a VIP. It touches their heart and makes them feel ignited for the whole day. They like and feel happy about it.

People ask me often, do you have a family business? I reply to them humbly "I don't have a family business but I run my business like my family" and that helps me and my business in many ways. The most important factor is that my team's attrition rate is the lowest in the industry. This is a dividend I enjoy when I touch people's life.

They feel happy and delighted. They feel like a VIP. They feel how much I love them, how much I care for them and respect them. In return, I get a great amount of gratitude, blessings and a positive image in their mind and heart. I build my Karma by making somebody feel very special and happy.

I still wish people on their birthdays and anniversaries even the ones who are not with me and have separated long ago due to various reasons.

They express their happiness and gratitude when I wish them.

They say "I was expecting your wishes first thing in the morning." In fact, I prefer to wish them early in the morning for two reasons. One- when I am among the first few to wish them, they remember my wishes for the entire day and second thing, I don't forget to wish them even after I am occupied in my daily office routines.

Sugandha Parab is a superwoman. She is a fountain of energy and a mountain of enthusiasm. She is my batchmate. We studied together almost thirty years ago. In 2018, we got reconnected through social media. We have a common group of our batchmates. In the last one year, I have noticed an incredible thing about her. She remembers to wish each and every member of this group on their birthdays and wedding anniversary without fail. I was highly impressed by her attention, involvement, dedication and commitment. However busy she is, she would be the first to wish everybody. What a Superwoman. When I asked her about this, she replied in a very polite manner "I love to do this. I love to wish people who are important to me." What a great thought. Simply amazing. Awesome is the only word to describe her.

You need to check how big your special list of people is, whom you wish on their special occasions. Bigger the list, bigger the joy of giving.

When you touch some body's life, you win their heart. When you win people and do not try to defeat them, you touch many lives. Winning the heart is a key thing.

> *"If you want to stand out in your life*
> *then do something outstanding."*
>
> **—Satessh Singh**

When you wish somebody on a special occasion, actually you not only become a great human being but also deposit a lot of **KARMA** in your **KARMA Bank**.

Making somebody feel special and happy is a very special experience. In today's world when the majority of people are busy in backbiting, if you do something good then that good deed gets converted into a great **KARMA.**

💡 GOLDEN NUGGETS

- *Every human being likes to be given importance. We love to be noticed, recognized and feel important when somebody treats us like a VIP.*

- *Dedicate your few minutes daily to wish people and make people feel like a VIP. It touches their heart and makes them feel ignited for whole day.*

- *I love to do this. I love to wish people who are important to me.*

- *You need to check how big is your special list of people whom you wish on their special occasions.*

- *When you touch somebody's life, you win their heart.*

- *If you want to stand out in your life then do something outstanding.*

CHAPTER

Twenty Two

Be a CPO -
Chief Purpose Officer

"To begin to think with purpose is to enter the ranks of those strong ones who only recognize the failure as one of the pathways to attainment."

—James Allen,
Author of the bestseller "As a Man Thinketh"

Let me tell you that the book "As a Man Thinketh" written by James Allen has changed my life forever. Every sentence in this book has the power to transform your life. I am highly influenced by it.

You need to find the real purpose of your life. Please do not get confused by your materialistic achievement and purpose of life. Though the materialistic world is highly important and critical but the purpose of our life is way above. The purpose of our life puts us in a different orbit.

You need to think and operate like a CPO- Chief Purpose Officer. You need to become a Chief Purpose Officer of your own life.

The purpose of life is not to be only happy and contended. It is to be useful. To be compassionate. To make a difference in people's life. The purpose of life should be to positively impact the life of many. The purpose of life should be to bring happiness in people's life who are around you. The purpose of life is not to please anybody, instead, adding value in people's life and bringing positive changes. You need to contribute towards society, nation, world and the entire Universe with your best of the capability.

Mother Theresa, Steve Jobs, Bill Gates, Martin Luther King Jr., JRD Tata and many more such people are known for their purposeful life. They have been the Chief Purpose Officers.

Do you have to become a millionaire or billionaire to become a Chief Purpose Officer? Of course not. Let those people be more purposeful by way of doing CSR- Corporate Social Responsibility activities but you can easily do by way of doing ISR- Individual Social Responsibility. Contribute to the betterment of the society, nation and world in whatever way you can do it.

"The purpose of life is not to be happy. It is to be useful, to be compassionate, to make some difference that you have lived and lived well."

—Ralph Waldo Emerson

Your life must have a purpose. Your story is important. Your dreams count. Your inner voice matters. You were born to make an impact. Check your abundance list. Find a purpose and how you can add value, how you can impact somebody's life positively.

Your purpose is not only to do the 9 am to 6 pm shift work and bring a particular paycheck but your purpose should be what value you can add in other people's life. How best you can contribute.

*"The meaning of life is to find your gift and
purpose of life is to give it away."*

—Pablo Picasso

A purposeful life is not about being rich, being popular, being highly educated or being materialistic. It's about being real, being humble, being able to impact the lives of others. Life without a purpose is like a body without a soul.

Manjari Upadhyay is a successful corporate manager and doing a great amount of purposeful work in Central UP for the upliftment of the society. She founded Jijiwisha Society along with some like-minded individuals that works on the doctrine of Welfare State which advocates about the 'maximum happiness for maximum people'. Jijiwisha Society is contributing in the field of environmental justice to meet the survival crisis by way of plantation and maintenance of 3500 plus trees and recycling old clothes into bags to make a plastic-free society. Jijiwisha Society is also working and contributing in the field of Education, Healthcare, Sports and treating the underprivileged as a part of the mainstream world. She has a tremendous mindset of giving back to the society. Salute to her mindset, efforts and never-giving-up attitude which she takes pride to deliver her purpose of life. It is said well start is half done. Manjari is a true CPO – Chief Purpose Officer. She is adding value to society. She is positively impacting people's life. She is doing something which is extraordinary and outstanding. She is an extraordinary human being.

When you look at your surroundings, you would find many Chief Purpose Officers who are impacting the society in a big way. They keep inspiring and motivating us to become one among them.

But then we are scared of becoming a Chief Purpose Officer. We strongly believe in the happy-go-lucky attitude. We are prisoners of our purposeless life. We are more involved and engaged in our routine directionless life. We are absolutely self-centered.

I am not saying you should not earn money or not create wealth or not enjoy your materialistic world but at the same time, you can have a purposeful life too. The purpose of life will give huge accomplishment and satisfaction.

So, find what the purpose of your life is.

I am sure you would love to become a CPO- Chief Purpose Officer.

💡 GOLDEN NUGGETS ———————————

- *You need to find the real purpose of your life*

- *Become a CPO- Chief Purpose Officer of your own life*

- *The purpose of life is not to be only happy and contended. It is to be useful. To be compassionate. To make a difference in people's life*

- *The purpose of life should be to positively impact the life of many. The purpose of life should be to bring happiness in people around you*

- *Contribute for the betterment of the society, nation and world in whatever way you can do it*

- *Your life must have a purpose. Your story is important. Your dreams count. Your inner voice matters*

- *You were born to make an impact. Check your abundance list. Find a purpose how can you add value, how can you impact somebody's life positively*

- *The life without a purpose is like a body without a soul*

- *We are prisoners of our purposeless life. We are more involved and engaged in our routine directionless life*

- *The purpose of life will give a sense of huge accomplishment and satisfaction*

CHAPTER
Twenty Three

Skill Would Pay your Bills

How true is this?

Skills, when applied, make us an achiever. We can achieve great things this way.

> *"A man must develop a WILL and SKILLS to*
> *achieve great milestones in his life."*

—Satessh Singh

The mindset of average people follows the ideology of doing less and expecting more whereas the extraordinary people believe in doing more and achieving more. Ordinary people are daydreamers. They only dream and dream and dream. But extraordinary people always combine action and deadline with their dreams. A dream should be combined with a definite action plan.

We have been taught and conditioned to think big and dream big but nobody taught us why to think big. How to think big? And how to make it happen? Majority of the time people don't know the "how" part which is the 'skill" area. Knowing is not doing; taking the action is doing.

When a student studies pharmacy, he is taught how to prepare medicine. When a student does his medicine course, he is trained on how to diagnose and treat a patient. An architect is taught the basics about the architectural science and art of execution.

What about handling the challenges of life or challenges of building a career? Rarely these skills are taught therefore a person always struggles and gets frustrated.

When we teach people by equipping them with the required skills, they start liking the task and when they get success, their confidence builds up like never before.

Confidence gives success and success further boosts confidence which is a vicious cycle. Similarly, poor confidence leads to poor success and poor success further results in poor confidence. So, the initial confidence is the critical component to ensure success.

Now, from where does a man get this confidence. By having knowledge? Of course not. Because knowledge is available in abundance on social media and public domains. The most important element is skill. Skill is the only thing that teaches oneself HOW to do anything effectively and efficiently. Once the skill is acquired and applied then the confidence level goes up. With increased confidence and acquired skills, the chances of getting success increase many fold.

> *"Getting opportunity is Providence*
> *but grabbing them is Diligence."*
>
> **—Satessh Singh**

Skills, not theories, make us rich. Skills need to be acquired and applied to bring success and laurels.

Rahul was our office assistant in one of my MNC companies where I served as a General Manager. He was good at housekeeping and back end office management. He used to be the first to check-in and the last man to check-out. All employees used to look out for him. He used to do every task in a seamless manner. He used to ensure zero error. The team of seventy-five employees was absolutely dependent on his services. He used to manage the banking services, ATM withdrawals, courier services, housekeeping in addition to running a contractual canteen. What a superman he was! He was the blue-eyed man of all the bosses. Absolutely an all-rounder man, always wearing a contagious smile. Salute to his attitude, skills and passion to do every task flawlessly. I was highly inspired by his attitude, knowledge, skills, passion, energy and charismatic personality. I wish he could have earned handsome money too.

How beautifully Albert Einstein had written, "Once you stop learning, you start dying."

💡 GOLDEN NUGGETS

- *We achieve something great when we apply skills*

- *A man must develop a WILL and SKILL to achieve great milestones in his life*

- *Extraordinary people always combine their drems with an action and deadline*

- *Confidence gives success and success further boosts confidence*

- *Poor confidence leads to poor success and poor success further results in poor confidence*

- *With increased confidence, the chances of getting success increases many fold*

- *Getting opportunity is Providence but grabbing them is Diligence*

- *Skills, not theories, make us rich. Applied knowledge and skills bring success and laurels*

- *Once you stop learning, you start dying*

CHAPTER
Twenty Four

Emotion is a Strength and NOT Weakness

Emotion is energy in motion. Energy can be positive or negative. Emotion is a physical reaction to a thought. If you can control your thought then you can control your emotions.

Many times, we are busy doing the over-analysis which leads to paralysis. As a human being, we love to anazlyze and sometimes we overdo it.

Emotion is a beautiful thing that makes us a better human being. The value of emotion comes from sharing them and not by holding them. Unexpressed emotions will never die. They are buried alive and will come forth later in an uglier way. So, better you express emotions.

As a human being, you need to master emotions. Be expressive but without hurting others. Never allow your emotions to overpower your intelligence.

Even anger is a valid emotion. It's only bad when it takes control and makes you do things you don't want to do. In fact, emotions are the language of the soul.

Feelings are like a visitor. Let them come and go. Treat emotions as a temporary state of mind. Don't let them permanently destroy you. Don't allow emotions to become a permanent resident inside you.

> *"If you can't control your emotions,*
> *you can't control your money."*
>
> **—Warren Buffet**

I have heard many people quoting themselves that they are highly emotional. Nothing wrong in being an emotional man. I don't think, in any way emotion can become a weakness. It's a physical reaction to a thought. It's a symbol of strength.

When you hear a good news; you laugh, you smile and you celebrate. This is a natural way to react to the positive news or event, similarly when you hear a sad news or come across some setback; you feel bad. This is absolutely a normal reaction.

I must have interviewed thousands of people in my 27 years of corporate career. Whenever I asked a candidate to share their weaknesses, almost 99% people said, "I am an emotional person." I fail to understand why they feel emotion is their weakness.

It is up to an individual how to use emotions, whether to use as a strength or as a weakness. It's a personal choice.

When candidates get rejected and don't get a job, they feel sad and when the same candidate gets selected with a handsome jump in their CTC, they are delighted. The same candidate exhibits two different emotions. Unhappy and happy are two different emotions for them.

I remember 28th April 1995 when for the first time I became a proud father of a sweet daughter. That was emotionally the happiest day of my life. The joy, the happiness, the sweet memories I still cherish even after twenty-three years. It was the biggest and happiest moment of my life. I was on cloud nine. Again, when I became a father for the second time on 31st December 2000, my son was born, I was thrilled with joy and happiness. I had the same kind of emotions. I loved and cherish both the events.

The above two occasions are a classic example of a positive emotion.

I lost my mother on 25th June 2014. I was highly sad, feeling low and depressed. That moment, I could see my entire time with her flash in front of my eyes. Both the good and the bad. Despite best efforts, we couldn't save her. It would be a great regret for me for the rest of my life.

Now, the departure of my mother is a classic example of a negative emotion.

Now, can I say any of above emotions are my weakness? Of course not. Because as a human being, we carry our positive and negative emotions based upon a particular situation, environment and event.

The critical point is that sometimes we like a few situations, so we are happy and sometimes we don't, so we are unhappy. We forget the happy moment very soon but we carry the sad moment for a long time. Whereas, one should do the reverse. Carry happy moments forever and treat them as a reference point to inspire yourself and forget the sad moment as earliest possible to move ahead. Earlier the better. Both positive and negative emotions hold great power. For only the negative emotions make us realise the true strength of positive emotions.

Please keep in mind "Life is a celebration and not a struggle so let's celebrate it."

"Negativity de-hydrates but positivity re-hydrates."

—Satessh Singh

Build positive emotions. Convert your emotion as your strength and not weakness. Create an aura of positivity around you. Let your positive emotion impact your surroundings. Let your positive emotion brighten up the lives of millions.

You and only you can control your emotions. Be absolutely balanced in your emotions. Feelings are like visitors. They come and go. Do we get carried away by the visitors in our life? Of course not. Handle emotions with utmost care.

GOLDEN NUGGETS

- *Emotion is energy in motion. Energy can be positive or negative*

- *Emotion is a physical reaction to a thought. If you can control your thought then you can control your emotions as well*

- *Emotion is a beautiful thing which makes us a better human being*

- *The value of emotion comes from sharing them and not by holding them*

- *Unexpressed emotions will never die. They are buried alive and will come forth later in a more uglier way. Better you express your emotions*

- *Never allow your emotions to overpower your intelligence*

- *Emotions are the language of the soul*

- *Feelings are like a visitor. Let them come and go*

- *If you can't control your emotions, you can't control your money*

- *Carry happy moments forever and treat them as a reference point to inspire yourself and forget the sad moments as earliest possible to move ahead. Earlier the better*

- *Life is a celebration and not a struggle, so let's celebrate it*

- *Negativity de-hydrates but positivity re-hydrates*

- *Let your positive emotion impact your surroundings. Let your positive emotion brighten up the lives of millions*

- *You and only you can control your emotions. Be absolutely balanced in your emotions*

CHAPTER
Twenty Five

Become a CCO -
Chief Caring Officer

Human life is the greatest gift to mankind.

Being caring allows you to have empathy for others and to live a life based on affection, love and compassion for the people around you.

Being caring means providing a listening ear and noticing when someone needs help and helping the society without expecting any reward.

You must feel empathy towards others. Empathy means caring and sharing. Empathy is ***DILL KI DAULAT*** (wealth of the heart).

When you care about somebody you must express through your actions. Let it be a small action but express through your action that you care for others. People have a misconception that care is only when something significant is done. No. it's not. Every small act of humanity must be expressed that confirms you care.

You all must be aware of the customer care center for products or services but unfortunately, you are always or majority of the time unhappy and disappointed to see a poor customer care approach by the service provider or a product seller.

As state earlier, management guru Philip Kotler beautifully mentioned that "the best advertising is done by satisfied customers".

Let us apply Philip Kotler's approach in our real life too. People whom we meet are actually our internal or external customers. If we are dealing with customers then there must be a "Customer Care Mindset" inside us. Whenever we are dealing with people around us, we must give utmost attention and care to them. Because these are the people who will give their testimonials for us. They would become a 'Brand Ambassador' for us. They will do advertising on our behalf and that too free of cost.

We need to treat people as our customers.

Are you thinking, acting and behaving like a CCO-Chief Caring Officer. Do you care for their likes and dislikes? Do you value their happiness? Are you making them delighted? Are they getting a feeling of being treated like a VIP? Are you caring about their need and wants? If your answer is yes then please pat yourself because you have earned yourself the position of CCO- Chief Caring Officer and if your answer is no then you are in deep trouble.

When you truly care for someone, their mistakes never change our feelings because it's the mind that gets angry but the heart still cares. Again, keep in mind that feelings are like visitors, they come and go. Feelings must be temporary.

Many times people say they care but you know we are always judged by our actions and not by words. When care is expressed honestly people can make out, people can feel it. One can't be fooled all the time. Be honest in your expressions. Don't be fake. Be real. Be authentic. Be honest.

Being caring means to have feelings like concern, responsibility and love for someone or something. The act of caring for others is so powerful because it creates deeper bonds as individuals lean on each other for emotional support.

The parents care for their children. Doctors and nurses care for their patients. The teachers care for their students. The families care for each other.

The companies care for their employees and customers. So if you notice, everyday we have an opportunity to extend a caring approach which will pay a rich dividend. One should genuinely feel happy to help. Caring is an attitude, a mindset.

Deb was an old and committed employee in one of the companies I have served where I was handling their India Domestic business. Due to sudden brain hemorrhage and a cardiac problem, he was hospitalized and the very next day he passed away. We all were in a deep shock. I remember he was a sales representative for almost two decades. Somehow, I could inspire and motivate him to take a promotion and within thirty-six months, he was again promoted for the second time. He was a tiger salesman. He left behind his wife and a daughter who had just completed her graduation. His untimely departure was highly upsetting and disturbing for all who were connected to him. Being the management head, I took charge of the situation and coordinated with my HR manager. We took a special approval from our Managing Director and settled his gratuity within few working days. I can still visualize that moment when I visited his home along with my HR Head and handed over the gratuity cheque to his family. They were in tears. It was a big relief for them at a time of the crucial situation. Had we done anything special? I don't think so. What we did was just an act of caring. Settling his account and handing over the amount within just seven days was a gesture of caring. Purely caring attitude and nothing else. We played the role of Chief Caring Officer.

I can narrate N-number of such incidences from my 27 years of corporate career where I tried to exhibit an example of Chief Caring Officer. I am sure you all must be better than me in your caring approach.

When we love, care and respect somebody, we must express it through our actions.

"We can't drive out the darkness but definitely we can turn on the lights."

—Satessh Singh

GOLDEN NUGGETS

- *Human life is the greatest gift to mankind*
- *Being caring means providing a listening ear and noticing when someone needs help and helping the society without expecting any reward*

- *You must feel empathy towards others. Empathy means caring and sharing. Empathy is DILL KI DAULAT (wealth of the heart)*

- *People whom we meet are actually our internal or external customers. If we are dealing with customers then there must be a "Customer Care Mindset" inside us*

- *Be honest in your expressions. Don't be fake. Be real. Be authentic. Be honest*

- *Caring is an attitude, a mindset*

- *When we love, care and respect somebody, we must express through our action*

- *We can't drive out the darkness but definitely we can turn on the lights*

CHAPTER
Twenty Six
Shift from NANO to PAPO

Don't be surprised to see words like NANO and PAPO.

You all know the meaning of these words which are practiced very often and routinely.

NANO is **N**egative **A**pproach **N**egative **O**utcome and **PAPO** is **P**ositive **A**pproach **P**ositive **O**utcome.

You know very well when we start any project or relation with a negative approach, we end up messing up and failing in the same. We don't create positivity around us. We are filled with many negative thoughts like "what if". This "what if" creates doubts, stigmas, low confidence, low interest level and thereby makes us attempt things halfheartedly. When we start dealing in a relationship or project or task with low self-esteem, low confidence and low interest level; we can't expect success, instead, chances of failure are very high.

In contrast to NANO, when we approach any relationship, project, task in a PAPO – Positive Approach Positive Outcome manner then the chances of success are very high.

If you think you are the winner then you will prove to be a winner but if you think you can't then definitely you can't make it.

When you close the doors of your mind to negative thoughts, the door of opportunity opens to you.

Napoleon Hill said, " Whatever the mind of a man can conceive and believe, it can achieve."

You are the master of your destiny. You can influence, direct, re-direct and control your own thought and environment. You can either break or make your life. You can make something out of nothing and you can make nothing out of something. So simple.

Developing a negative approach for anything and everything is very simple and common. As a human being, we easily get influenced by negativity but we take a lot of time to get influenced by positivity. We resist positivity. Success comes to those who are success-conscious. Failure comes to those who become failure conscious.

We need to learn the art of converting defeat into a stepping stone in order to succeed.

We need to learn how to bounce back. It is not important how deep we have fallen, but what is important, is how high we bounce back.

"Setback to comeback is called leadership."

—Satessh Singh

A positive approach is critical for a positive outcome. Input determines the output. Garbage in garbage out. We win a battle twice, once in our mind and second time in reality.

You must approach anything and everything with an open mind and an open heart.

Jack Ma, the founder of Alibaba says, " If you don't give up you still have a chance to win, hence don't give up."

Negative Approach leads to a Negative Outcome. Don't believe me? Try once and witness yourself.

Who can forget the Prudential Cricket World Cup 1983! For the first time India won a world cup under the captaincy of great Kapil Dev. I was in the seventh grade. I was not much knowledgeable about the cricket game at that time. In one of the interviews, (which was attended by Sunil Gavaskar, Kapil Dev, Mohinder Amarnath, Kirti Azad, Madan Lal and K.Srikkanth) I heard them discussing about how Kapil Dev, as a young captain of the Indian team, infused tremendous belief among all the Indian players that, 'let's give our best and enjoy the tour'. When India entered into the finals, in the dressing room Kapil Dev appealed to all players "Reaching to the finals itself is a big achievement for us, so let us go out and give our best." We all know the rest is history. Nobody could believe that Kapil's devils could defeat the giant army of Clive Lloyd. A classic example of **PAPO** - **P**ositive **A**pproach leads to **P**ositive **O**utcome.

We are always caged inside negativity. We prefer to give an excuse for our non-achievement. We love to earn the sympathy of others. We expose our emotions to win sympathy. Whereas emotion is energy in motion. It is up to us how to use it. We use positive emotions for positive outcomes and negative emotions for negative outcomes.

Does it make sense to remain in NANO? Or should we shift from NANO to PAPO? I would prefer to move from NANO to PAPO. Give your best and look forward to the best. Nothing lesser than the best.

"Today's accomplishments were yesterday's impossibilities."

—Dr. Robert H. Schuller

We develop the fear of failure, fear of what others would say. What if I don't succeed? These are all negative suggestions which we keep giving to our conscious and subconscious mind. What goes inside comes outside. Very simple. Then why to give a negative message and why not give the fodder of positivity to our mind.

Let us develop a positive mindset for ourselves. We have to become a highly influential personality so we need to train our mind to think positive and act positive to achieve positive.

💡 GOLDEN NUGGETS ─────────────

- *NANO is Negative Approach for Negative Outcome and PAPO is Positive Approach for Positive Outcome*

- *If you think you are the winner then you will prove to be a winner but if you think you can't then definitely you can't make it*

- *When you close the doors of your mind to negative thoughts, the door of opportunity opens to you*

- *Whatever the mind of a man can conceive and believe, it can achieve*

- *You are the master of your destiny. You can influence, direct, re-direct and control your own thought and environment*

- *You can either break or make your life. You can make something out of nothing and you can make nothing out of something*

- *We resist positivity*

- *Success comes to those who are success conscious. Failure comes to those become failure conscious*

- *We need to learn the art of converting defeat into a stepping stone for success*

- *It is not important how deep we have fallen but what is important is that how tall we are bouncing back*

- *We win a battle twice - once in our mind and second time in reality*

- *If you don't give up, you still have a chance to win, hence don't give up*

- *We are always caged inside negativity*

- *We love to earn sympathy of others. We expose our emotions to win sympathy*

- *Today's accomplishments were yesterday's impossibilities*

CHAPTER

Twenty Seven

Thinking is an Art

People believe that thinking is a God gifted talent. The truth is thinking is also a skill that can be developed and acquired by learning different techniques.

We will now learn about how thinking can be developed and mastered in our day-to-day life. You all know our brain has two different lobes. The right lobe and the left lobe.

The right brain is highly creative, imaginative, operates in present and future, philosophical, religious, fantasy-based, intuitive, subjective, boundary-less, spontaneous, full of possibilities and risk-taker, appreciative, understands symbols and images, responds to the feelings, big picture-oriented and is a big believer.

On the other hand, the left brain is calculative, factual, mathematical, scientific, operates in present and past, reality-based, rational, objective, within a boundary, practical, plays safe, understands words and languages, logical and detail-oriented.

The right brain controls the left part of the body and the left brain controls the right part.

The right nostril is solar and regulated by the sun and the left nostril is lunar and regulated by the moon.

People who breath-in and breath-out "slowly" are healthy and live for a longer time. People who breath-in and breath-out fast have a poor health status. They struggle to remain healthy for the rest of their life. The classic examples are tortoises and dogs. Tortoise breathes slowly hence they live for 300 to 400 years and dogs breathe very fast hence they live just for up to ten years only (some exceptions).

We should breathe slowly on a pattern of 4-6-4. Count 4 while breathing-in then hold for 6 counts and breath-out while counting till 4. This is an ideal way to breath-in, hold and then breath-out. When a person is angry his/her breathing becomes very fast and just opposite to this is when a person sleeps the breathing becomes slow and normal.

We can practice 5 S.T.A.A.R Thinking Formula to become highly conscious and alert in our thinking and decision making. The 5 S.T.A.A.R Thinking Formula is highly scientific and based on the characteristics of our Right and Left brain.

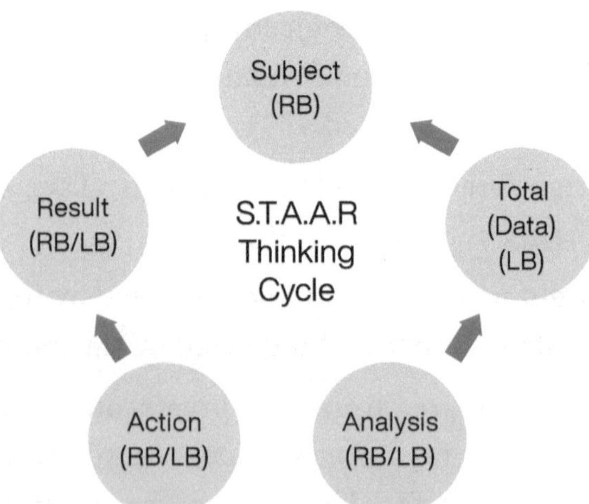

S.T.A.A.R. Thinking Formula starts with **Subject** which is handled by the Right brain. The right brain is highly **Sub**jective in nature. T is **Tr**uth based which is data-based and the same is handled by the Left Brain. **A** is **A**nalytical which is handled by our Left Brain because our left brain is calculative in nature so it does all the processing job. **A** is **A**ctionable decision where a lot of creativity is required and the Right brain being a creative brain, does it very well. Finally, **R** stands for **R**esult for which we need to use a blend of Right and Left brain as it involves creative and calculative brains, both.

In our brain, the Pre-frontal cortex stimulates "THINKING".

It further changes behavior and finally brings motivation to an individual. The brain releases dopamine, serotonin and endorphins. These hormones stimulate "good and happy" feelings thereby reducing "pain and anxiety".

The pre-frontal cortex is involved in self-motivation. Motivation comes from (a) Intrinsic factors & (b) Extrinsic factors.

Intrinsic factor comes from internal stimuli which is self-charging. Intrinsic motivation is long-lasting and purposeful.

Extrinsic factor comes from external stimuli which needs external charging. Extrinsic motivation lasts for a short period and is non-purposeful.

There are various factors and ways by which we can activate our thinking. I wish to mention a few significant tips here to help you.

The most important factors that activate our thinking are: 1. Aroma or smell, 2. Swar Vidya (Science of breathing) & 3. Food

1. An aroma or smell plays a critical and vital role to activate our thinking ability. Aroma is very important in the activation of our brain. Our all other sensory information takes time to get into the brain whereas aroma/smell goes directly into the Limbic system onto the cortex and thereby it stimulates our thinking.

   Studies have shown that good aroma or smell increases memories. A very interesting report mentions that women have a much more sensitive sense of smell than men.

2. The regular practice of SWAR VIDYA (Science of breathing) helps in the activation of our thinking abilities. If daily in the morning we practice SWAR VIDYA for five minutes, we can reboot and refresh our brain and condition it to think fast and think clear. The right brain controls the left part of the body and the left brain controls the right part of the body. Breath-in and breath-out through the left nostril activates the right brain and breath-in and breath-out through the right nostril activates

the left brain. This is called "SWAR VIDYA", the science of breathing.

3. Food for thought: There are specific foods which can help us to improve our thinking abilities. To name a few among fruits are banana, apple, watermelon and among vegetables are red beet, cucumber, beans, legumes and soybeans. The balanced and moderate consumption of dark chocolates, cheese, walnuts, honey and green tea can also help in the activation of our thinking.

William Shakespeare says that "there is nothing either good or bad but thinking makes it so".

 GOLDEN NUGGETS

- *The right brain is highly creative, imaginative, operates in the present and future, philosophical, religious, fantasy based, intuitive, subjective, boundary-less, spontaneous, full of possibilities and risk taker*

- *The left brain is calculative, factual, mathematical, scientific, operates in present and past, reality based, rational, objective, within a boundary, practical and plays safe*

- *The right brain controls the left part of the body and left brain controls the right part of the body*

- *The right nostril is solar and regulated by the sun and left nostril is lunar and regulated by the moon*

- *People who breath-in and breath-out "slowly" are healthy and live for a longer time*

- *People who breath-in and breath-out very fast have a poor health status*

- *We should breathe slowly on a pattern of 4-6-4. Count 4 while breathing-in then hold for 6 counts and breath-out by counting 4*

- *When a person is angry, the breathing becomes very fast and opposite to this is when a person sleeps, the breathing becomes slow and normal*

- *Brain releases dopamine, serotonin and endorphins. These hormones stimulate "good and happy" feelings thereby reduce "pain and anxiety"*

- *Intrinsic factor comes from internal stimuli which is self-charging. Intrinsic motivation is long lasting and purposeful*

- *Extrinsic factor comes from external stimuli which needs external charging. Extrinsic motivation lasts for a short period and is non-purposeful*

CHAPTER
Twenty Eight
Practice Positive Affirmation

A positive affirmation in the new age refers to the practice of positive thinking and self-empowerment. Fostering a belief that a positive mental attitude supported by affirmations will achieve success in anything and everything.

A positive affirmation is a carefully formatted statement that should be repeated to one's self and written down frequently. For affirmations to be effective, they need to be in the present tense, positive, personal and very specific.

The proponents of affirmations say that "with our thoughts, desires and emotions, we can create our world".

For any affirmation to work effectively it has to have:

(a) Visualization of the affirmations

(b) Emotional feelings attached to it &

(c) Vocalization of the affirmation with a minimum hundred percentage of belief, confidence and faith.

Affirmations work best when it is combined with acknowledgments. A study done in the year 2009 suggests that positive affirmations had a positive effect on people who had very high self-esteem and in contrast to this had a detrimental effect on those with low self-esteem.

Some very interesting studies also found that self-affirmations involve writing about one's core values rather than repeating. A positive self-statement can improve performance under stress.

One needs to practice the positive affirmation technique to manifest greater aspirations and dreams. One needs to have a 3V approach (1) Visualization (2) Verbalisation & (3) Vitalization with a great degree of emotions, belief, and a sense of gratitude.

The repetition of positive affirmation leads to a positive belief. Once this belief becomes a deep conviction then things begin to happen. Therefore, belief is a critical ingredient to fulfil the manifestation.

A positive affirmation opens the door to bring positive change.

Our mind is a powerful thing. When we fill it with positive thoughts, our life changes completely.

When we practice positive affirmations, we tell the Universe what we want to manifest and then all the positive energy present in the Universe starts helping and supporting us. We seek and we get it. So simple.

The way we think, we create. What we feel, we attract and finally what we imagine, we become. It's a mental game for sure.

We need to create a mental image in our mind. Our life is in our hands. No matter where we are now. No matter what has happened in our life. When we visualize, verbalize and vitalize we fulfill our dreams.

When we focus our thoughts on something very specific which we want and if we hold our focus on that particular thought, then we are in that moment with our strong desire. Thereby, the Universe helps us to achieve our dreams and aspirations.

GOLDEN NUGGETS

- *A positive affirmation is a carefully formatted statement that should be repeated to one's self and written down frequently*

- *For affirmations to be effective, they need to be in present tense, positive, personal and very specific*

- *Affirmations work best when they are is combined with acknowledgements*

- *A positive self-statement can improve performance under stress*

- *A positive affirmation opens the door to bring a positive change*

- *We need to create a mental image in our mind*

CHAPTER
Twenty Nine

The Power of Imagination

Imagination is the ability to form a mental image of something that is not perceived through our five senses. It is the ability of our mind to build mental scenes, objects or events that do not exist or are not present or have occurred in the past.

The ability to imagine things pervades our entire existence. It influences everything that we do, think about and create. It leads to elaborate theories, dreams and inventions in any profession from the realms of academia to engineering and the arts.

Imagination enhances your problem-solving skills.

Being imaginative in your leisure time can also help you overcome obstacles at work.

Imagination has much to do with reality. It shapes the way we see our reality and therefore affects our expectations and hopes, our actions and behavior.

It's believed that imagination involves a network that helps to share information across different regions of the brain. These different regions work together to form mental images in our head.

The logical thinking can take you from point A to point B but imaginative thinking will take you to many places, from point A to B and beyond.

We can create anything if we can develop the ability to imagine. Whether aeroplane, telephone, camera, internet, cellular phone, radio cab services, online shopping platforms or any other product or services which has disrupted and positively impacted the world is an outcome of imaginary power.

When we imagine something which doesn't exist today, we may become a subject of laughter in the society. People tease or taunt us behind our back because they can't see what we can see and imagine. It's perfectly fine if they laugh at us. Because they don't know how the future can be impacted by our imagination. In the past, people never believed a man can fly, talk over the phone while sitting at some distance or run a business through some virtual platform. Today, all these things are possible because somebody at some point in time dared to imagine.

"Today's imagination would become tomorrow's reality."

—Satessh Singh

People who have the courage to imagine would certainly create an impact in the world. They would become the game-changer. One needs to become shameless to become a great personality through their power of imagination. One needs to have the courage, passion, attitude and a mindset to imagine which nobody else could dare to do.

While imagining something which is non-existential, we need not give attention to the negative people who don't believe in us. Instead, we should focus on the outcome and impact that we are going to create through our power of imagination. Let us not abort our vision because of someone else's mission to derail our dream. Keep going and keep growing.

The human imagination works in its own way. The main factor is natural intelligence. We give too much importance to artificial intelligence but a human being's natural intelligence only gave birth to artificial intelligence. There are two ways how imagination works. One by way of 'Synthetic imagination' and other by way of 'Creative imagination'.

In synthetic imagination, we arrange some old concepts, old ideas and an old formula to create something new. By using and applying synthetic imagination along with our past observations, experiences, education, knowledge and skills we can give shape and form to our idea and become highly successful.

In creative imagination, we work automatically. Creative imagination flows naturally. Creative imagination is highly powerful and impactful. All great leaders in all walks of life whether in business, arts, science, sports, entertainment industry or any other field who have disrupted the world with their breakthrough products or services have used the power of their creative imagination.

To achieve our aspirations and dreams, we must use the power of our creative imagination.

💡 GOLDEN NUGGETS

- *Imagination enhances your problem-solving skills*

- *Being imaginative in your leisure time can also help you overcome obstacles at work*

- *The logical thinking can take you from point A to point B but imaginative thinking will take you to many places*

- *We can create anything if we can develop the ability to imagine*

- *Today's imagination would become tomorrow's reality*

- *There are two ways how imagination works. One by way of 'Synthetic imagination' and other by way of 'Creative imagination'*

- *To achieve our aspirations and dreams, we must use the power of our creative imagination*

CHAPTER
Thirty

Turbocharge Yourself

Today's world is full of negativity. Right from the time we wake up till the time we retire on bed, we face negativity. The moment we switch on TV early in the morning to watch some news channel, we see a lot many negative news across the world. When we open the daily newspaper, we see many negative events. We start our day with loads of negativity. As the day keeps progressing, we keep getting negative inputs which in turn affect our brain. By the time we are back home, we are already polluted and contaminated with various negativity.

The best way to turbocharge yourself is by investing the first sixty minutes in an *MBBS Spa*. The moment we get up early in the morning, we need to invest our first hour to prepare our mind, body, business and soul.

Visit an "MBBS Spa" early in the morning at home or hotel wherever you are. The **MBBS Spa** means **M**ind, **B**ody, **B**usiness and **S**oul Spa. We must take an MBBS Spa first thing in the morning.

You must follow the 15:15:15:15 Concept to turbocharge yourself by visiting the MBBS Spa.

When you wake up, you need to invest the first fifteen minutes practicing a simple meditation in which you can simply close your eyes and focus on the center part of your forehead. Simply close both of your eyes and focus on the third eye area which is situated in between the eyes;

just above the nose. Feel relaxed and focused on the third eye point by bringing back all your thoughts and trying to be in trance. Be cool, be calm and relax your body. Set an alarm for fifteen minutes. Open your eyes after fifteen minutes and you feel absolutely relaxed and relieved.

Meditation is the tongue of the soul and the language of our spirit.

"Meditation means dissolving the invisible walls that unawareness has built."

—Sadhguru

The second set of fifteen minutes must be invested to train your body by doing some kind of exercise. Many people think and feel that exercise can be done only in gyms. That's not the truth. The simplest way of doing a physical exercise is to walk for fifteen minutes early in the morning. For a fifteen-minute walk, one needs only a pair of sports shoes. That's it. Walk daily without a gap. Consistency is the key.

"Embrace and love your body. It's the most amazing thing you'll ever own."

—Anonymous

The third set of fifteen minutes must be invested to take care of your business (work-related). Take a paper and a pen and make a 'to do list' for the day based on your priority and importance. Keep only those chores for yourself which need your personal intervention and decision-making. Please do not hijack somebody else's miscellaneous work. Never downgrade your role play. You may get tempted to do many non-important chores which can be done by your juniors or subordinates. The "to do list" must be well-thought of and well-planned. Please ensure that you DO NOT deviate from your original "to do list" unless and until something urgent or emergency work comes in your way. This fifteen-minute allocation is adequate to plan and design your "to do list".

"He who fails to plan is planning to fail."

—Winston Churchill

Now, the last set of fifteen minutes must be invested to uplift your soul. This is the time zone when we must read something that would add infinite value to our soul. We can read some spiritual books like Bhagwad Gita, Ramayana, Quran, Bible, autobiographies or any self-help book. Remember, reading is the food for our soul. Input would decide the output. When we consume great thoughts, we can exhibit those great thoughts in our day-to-day life. If we read negative news then our soul would get polluted and contaminated accordingly. But if we read something positive then for the entire day our soul creates an aura that would create a positive environment around us.

"Books give a soul to the universe, wings to the mind, flight to the imagination and life to everything."

—Plato

After having sixty minutes of an MBBS Spa now you are turbocharged for the day. You are now prepared to face all the adversities of the world. You are ready to absorb all kinds of shocks and challenges that the world will throw at you. You are ready to overcome any kind of obstacle. Now, you are ready to roar, outperform and enjoy your work-life balance.

Once you are done with your MBBS Spa, you are highly energetic for the entire day. You radiate positive aura around you. Your face starts glowing. When you are highly energetic you make people around you also highly energetic. You spread positivity around your surrounding. Everywhere the environment is electrifying. People are turbocharged to deliver in surplus.

Once you come back from your workplace in a happy mood then not only are you turbocharged but your family members are also turbocharged. Whether its office or home, everywhere the atmosphere is like a festival and celebration. Now, you are in a turbocharging mode.

💡 GOLDEN NUGGETS

- *The best way to turbocharge yourself is by investing first sixty minutes in an MBBS Spa*

- *Meditation is the tongue of the soul and the language of our spirit*

- *Meditation means dissolving the invisible walls that unawareness has built*

- *Embrace and love your body. It's the most amazing thing you will ever own*

- *He who fails to plan is planning to fail*

- *Books give a soul to the universe, wings to the mind, flight to the imagination and life to everything*

CHAPTER
Thirty One
Re-Invent Yourself

Many of us have lost our passion, dream, childhood energy because we got overburdened by our personal and professional responsibilities.

You all had a great natural talent in you when you were a child. Many of you were an artist, singer, painter, actor, writer, scientist (we used to do many creative works in the childhood) and visualizers when you were a child. Over the period of time, all your childhood talent and passion got eclipsed or hijacked by your family responsibilities or/ and career responsibilities.

When I interviewed almost five hundred plus people and asked them about their passion, I found that hardly ten percentage of people are building their career around their passion. Rest all ninety percentage of people are living a career aspired and influenced by their parents or surroundings. Are they happy, satisfied and enjoying their career? Of course not because their aspirations were something else during their childhood. They adopted their parent's aspirations and started building the same. They are in a trap.

How do you handle this kind of challenge in your life? The answer is, you need to revisit your childhood. You need to go back and refer to what was exciting and inspiring to you. The hobbies or passion which you had forgotten and buried, now need to be revived slowly and gradually without affecting your current assignments.

You need to devote some time during the weekends to revive your old forgotten hobbies and passion that will rebuild your future. On weekends or Sundays, you can spend a few hours to rebuild your passion and hobby. I can assure you the amount of happiness, satisfaction and accomplishment you would get would be greater than what you are recieving today.

I call it converting "**passion into a profession**". Slowly and gradually, you can convert your passion into a new profession thereby you can also build your second source of income.

I am not saying to cheat with your current employer but parallel if you can build your second source of income then you can make your second source of income as the primary source of income which you would enjoy throughout your life.

One need not be busy 9 am to 6 pm to run his life- that is so monotonous.

Life is not a struggle, it's a celebration, so celebrate it.

Live life kingsize. When you don't refer to your wristwatch while checking-in and checking-out of your office that's an indication that you are not in a job but you are inside the job. Being in a job and being inside the job makes a great difference. When you forget time while working that's a proof that you are enjoying and celebrating your career.

Never follow a Punch Lunch and Punch (PLP Concept) Concept.

Today, I want you to commit to yourself that gradually you will reinvent your childhood hobbies and passion. Take a baby step today to build a greater tomorrow. Initially, it would be a little difficult to start but gradually you would catch up fast. Very soon you will master the same as it's your hobby and passion and not a job. It is your passion which you are converting into a profession, very soon.

Congratulations! Here your new journey starts "from a passion to a profession". Enjoy the journey and celebrate your passion.

Pursuing a career which you love and you are passionate about is like having an anti-aging pill on a daily basis. You won't face the aging problem. I guarantee. Many have done it and you can also do it. Thinking is not doing but doing is doing so let us do it.

Other best way to have a healthy and happier life is to re-connect with your school and college friends with whom you used to enjoy a lot. The old friends are the best stress-busters. You can connect with them through facebook or through some common friends who are still in touch with them and keep connecting through the phone or can meet in person once in six months. They have many success and setback stories to share with you and so you can also share your stories.

Believe me, connecting with old friends is highly therapeutic and refreshing.

Another way of enjoying a happy life is going on a holiday. Always take out some time to go on a holiday along with your family.

A family that spends time together lives together. Today, families hardly find any time to bond and go on a picnic. Holiday need not be a big one. Holiday need not be on a great location. Even one-day picnic will also help you to know each other better and bond with each other better. Bonding is necessary. Even a daytime picnic refreshes very well.

Ashish is a digital marketing manager. His wife is working for a big MNC consultancy company. They are a young couple and have been married for a few years now. They make it a point to go on domestic and international holidays once in six months. Once in six months they go for a domestic holiday and once in six months they go for an international vacation. What a way to celebrate their togetherness. God bless them with better and better holidays in the coming days too.

A family holiday relaxes, unwinds and brings us closer.

Travel is the only thing you buy that makes you richer.

💡 GOLDEN NUGGETS ─────────────────────

- *Hardly ten percentage people are building their career around their passion*

- *Ninety percentage people are living a career aspired and influenced by their parents or surroundings*

- *Life is not a struggle, it's a celebration, so celebrate it*

- *Live life kingsize*

- *Enjoy the journey and celebrate your passion*

- *Pursuing a career which you love and you are passionate about is like having an anti-ageing pill on a daily basis*

- *The old friends are the best stress-busters*

- *Connecting with old friends is highly therapeutic and refreshing*

- *Family that spends time together lives together.*

- *A family holiday relaxes, unwinds and brings us close and together.*

- *Travel is the only thing you buy that makes you richer.*

CHAPTER
Thirty Two

A list of Life-Changing Self-Help Books

I had promised earlier in this book that I would enlist some of the great self-help books which you can read, refer or suggest to your near and dear ones. Here is a list of fifteen authors and twenty books which have had a massive impact on me. I hope these books would create a big positive influence in your life too.

Here I go . . .

Author #1 *Dr. Robert Schuller*

1. Tough Times Never Last but Tough People Do

2. Success is Never Ending, Failure is Never Final

Author # 2 *James Allen*

1. As a Man Thinketh

2. Mind is The Master

Author #3 *Rhonda Byrne*

1. Secret

2. The Magic

Author #4 *Dale Carnegie*

1. How to Win Friends and Influence People

2. How to Stop Worrying and Start Living

Author #5 *Napoleon Hill*

1. Think and Grow Rich

2. The Law of Success

Author #6 *Wayne Dyer*

1. Change Your Thoughts – Change Your Life

Author #7 *Shiv Khera*

1. You Can Win

Author #8 *Paulo Coelho*

1. The Alchemist

Author #9 *Robin Sharma*

1. Monk Who Sold His Ferrari
2. The Greatness Guide

Author #10 *Norman Vincent Peale*

1. The Power of Positive Thinking
2. Stay Alive All Your Life

Author #11 *Dr Radhakrishnan Pillai*

1. Corporate Chanakya
2. Chanakya in You

Author #12 *David Schwartz*

1. The Magic of Thinking BIG

Author #13 *Dr. Spencer Johnson*

1. Who Moved My Cheese
2. Fish

Author #14 *Dr. Joseph Murphy*

1. The Power of Your Subconscious Mind
2. Believe in Yourself

Author #15 *Tony Robbins*

1. Awaken The Giant Within

Gratitude

I am happy and delighted that you have read my book. I hope your experience of reading this book was good, if not great.

My sincere gratitude. I hope and wish you must have liked a few concepts or chapters from this book. I would request you to make the best use of your experience from this book in your day-to-day life.

You can also gift your personal copy to someone whom you love the most by putting your own autograph on the first page of the book. You are my ambassador .

Please share some of the concepts mentioned in the book among your colleagues, family members, friends, relatives and customers so that they also can get benefitted.

I have taken the best possible precaution to avoid any technical or content errors but in case if you find something very critical please bring into my notice by writing an email.

I am a big CLO-Chief Listening Officer so I would love to listen to your suggestions and feedback. Please keep sharing.

I would love to listen from you about the book "How to Become a Highly Influential Personality" on my e-mail ID *satesshsingh@gmail.com*

Please drop a sentence about your feedback and response about the book. You may also drop your contact details so that I can revert. I promise to check and acknowledge each and every mail which I would receive.

Please also visit my website *www.satesshsingh.com*

Please look forward to the launch of my next business book very soon!

My sincere gratitude. God bless you forever.

Positively charged!

Satessh Singh
"How to become a Highly Influential Personality"

Page of Fame

I am thankful to you as you bought my book "How to Become a Highly Influential Personality".

Please share your **selfie pic along with the book** on the customer care manager's WhatsApp no.: +91-9529194308 or mail me directly on my mail ID: *satesshsingh@gmail.com*

I would love to design a collage-wall of all pictures and would print in the next edition of the book.

Last but not the least . . . .

If you like the "How to Become a Highly Influential Personality" book and got inspired by the contents and messages and wish to help others then please gift my book to your family members, friends, relatives, colleagues and people whom you want to help and develop as a highly influential personality.

Please share your thoughts and feedback about this book on Twitter, Facebook and Instagram or write a book review. It would help millions to reach out to my book.

If you are a manager or owner of a business then you can gift this book to your team members to improve their personality and performance. You can also gift this book on special occasions like birth anniversaries and wedding anniversaries or on promotions.

You can contact me at *satesshsingh@gmail.com* or visit my website wwww.satesshsingh.com

Positively Charged!

Satessh Singh
#1 Amazon Bestseller Author
"How to Become a Highly Influential Personality"